Stress-Free Potty Training

Geraldine Butler and
Bernice Walmsley

W9-DGG-128

For UK order enquiries: please contact Bookpoint Ltd,
130 Milton Park, Abingdon, Oxon OX14 4SB.
Telephone: +44 (0) 1235 827720. *Fax*: +44 (0) 1235 400454.
Lines are open 09.00–17.00, Monday to Saturday, with a 24-hour
message answering service. Details about our titles and how to
order are available at www.teachyourself.com

For USA order enquiries: please contact McGraw-Hill Customer
Service, PO Box 545, Blacklick, OH 43004-0545, USA.
Telephone: 1-800-722-4726. *Fax*: 1-614-755-5645.

For Canada order enquiries: please contact McGraw-Hill
Ryerson Ltd, 300 Water St, Whitby, Ontario L1N 9B6, Canada.
Telephone: 905 430 5000. *Fax*: 905 430 5020.

Long renowned as the authoritative source for self-guided learning –
with more than 50 million copies sold worldwide – the **Teach Yourself**
series includes over 500 titles in the fields of languages, crafts, hobbies,
business, computing and education.

British Library Cataloguing in Publication Data: a catalogue record
for this title is available from the British Library.

Library of Congress Catalog Card Number: on file.

First published in UK 2008 by Hodder Education, part of
Hachette Livre UK, 338 Euston Road, London, NW1 3BH.

First published in US 2008 by the McGraw-Hill Companies, Inc.

This edition published 2010.

The **Teach Yourself** name is a registered trade mark of
Hodder Headline.

Typeset by MPS Limited, A Macmillan Company.

Printed in Great Britain for Hodder Education, a Hachette UK
Company, 338 Euston Road, London NW1 3BH, by Cox &
Wyman Ltd, Reading, Berkshire.

The publisher has used its best endeavours to ensure that the URLs
for external websites referred to in this book are correct and active
at the time of going to press. However, the publisher and the
authors have no responsibility for the websites and can make no
guarantee that a site will remain live or that the content will remain
relevant, decent or appropriate.

Hachette UK's policy is to use papers that are natural, renewable
and recyclable products and made from wood grown in sustainable
forests. The logging and manufacturing processes are expected to
conform to the environmental regulations of the country of origin.

Impression number   10 9 8 7 6 5 4 3 2 1
Year   7316   2014 2013 2012 2011 2010

This book is dedicated to the Breast Cancer Services team at the Whittington Hospital in North London.

....

Acknowledgements

Both authors would like to thank the *Teach Yourself* team at Hodder for their friendly help and guidance.

Thanks from Geraldine Butler go to her husband, Paul, and daughters, Saskia and Portia, for all their help and support during the writing of this, her first book.

Bernice Walmsley would like to thank her husband, William, for his continuing support and encouragement.

Contents

Meet the authors

Welcome to *Stress-Free Potty Training*!

Toilet training is not just about a child being able to wee and poo in a potty. It is about so much more, including preparing your child well to enable him to learn this new skill. This will ensure that training is done quickly and is an enjoyable, fun event for child and parent alike. It is also about ensuring your child has the skills to become independent with toileting. This includes reacting to the cues his body will give him when he needs to empty his bowels or bladder, being able to dress and undress as needed, being able to wipe himself and knowing how to wash his hands properly after using the toilet.

The beauty of this book is that, unlike any other book on the market, it will travel with you along the whole of the toilet training journey – from deciding (using the toilet readiness questionnaire) that your child is ready, through all the preparation, to undertaking the whole training process. This book will support you and your child with any difficult phases that you may go through. It will support you with night-time training and preparing your child for starting school with those all-important, independent toileting skills. In addition, if you are encountering difficulties such as night-time wetting or your child has special needs then there are useful, informative sections for you.

Please note that when referring to your child, we have alternated the pronouns 'he' and 'she' in each chapter. This has been done for convenience only, and not because the chapters are gender-specific in any way.

Only got a minute?

When potty training your child, timing is probably one of the most important aspects in ensuring that training goes well. So, what do we mean by timing? It is not simply a question of your child being ready (having all the skills in place), although that is, of course, important. It is also about the timing being correct in terms of what is happening both in your child's life and in yours as a parent. Let us look at these issues in a little more detail.

You cannot toilet train your child successfully unless he has the skills in place. He needs the physical skill of being able to hold on to his wee for long enough to get to the potty, the understanding that when he gets the urge to wee he needs to sit on the potty, the skill to communicate this need to you and the self-help skills of being able to pull down his pants to sit on the potty. Only when he has all these skills in place is the time right.

You also need to get the timing right in terms of what is happening in his life. So, if there are any major life changes happening – for example, a new baby in the family, starting nursery or changing childcare, going on holiday or moving house – then it is best to delay training until the event has passed and life is more settled for him.

Timing is also important for you as a parent. The training needs to happen when you have the time to focus on it and give it the attention that it needs. So, if you work outside the home you may decide to take a week or so off work to do the bulk of the training in. If you are generally at home with your child you need to pick a time when you can have a quiet week to do the training in.

5 Only got five minutes?

Once you have decided that your child has the skills in place and the time is right, sort out the equipment that you will need:

▶ Two potties, one for the bathroom and one for the room you will use most. Buy both the same colour so there is no game playing about which colour potty to sit on.
▶ A child-size toilet seat with a small stool if your child is not keen to use the potty.
▶ Pants or pull-ups.
▶ Plenty of clothes that are easy to pull down and up.

Next decide when you are going to start. You need to make sure you scale down the week's activities so that you and your child can concentrate on the job in hand. Talk to your child and let him know what is expected to happen.

You are now ready to start. So, on the first day, after breakfast, it's off with the nappy. You may want to put on pants or a pull-up. Watch out for signs that your child needs a wee or a poo. If nothing has happened after one to one and a half hours pop your child on the potty. It does not matter if he does nothing – the most important thing is that he is happy to sit on the potty. Give him lots of praise even if he does nothing. You will need to keep popping him on the potty about every hour and a half. Whenever he has a success make a big fuss and he will soon make the connection that this is what he is expected to do. Keeping a diary can be helpful as it can pinpoint any changes that you need to make to the routine. Note that all children have accidents at first. Try not to get upset, just clean him up and then get on with life.

Bath time is often a good time to talk about your day. Have a little chat about any successes that he has had, and don't mention the accidents. This gives you another opportunity to praise him.

If your child is a little older – perhaps two and a half to three years old – an incentive such as a star chart with small rewards can work wonders.

You should be well on your way now but if you do find things are not falling into place, it may be worth taking a step back and popping your child back into nappies for a month and then trying again. There is nothing wrong in doing this. If there are still lots of accidents and few successes your child is not ready.

Once your child is making progress you can begin to think about going out without a nappy. Some preparation is needed for this. You may decide to buy a portable toilet to take with you. Make sure your child has had the opportunity to use the potty before going out and keep the trip short. Go somewhere where there will be a toilet or potty, or where you will be able to use the portable toilet. Explain to your child that you are going out without a nappy and that he needs to let you know if he needs a wee or poo.

Some children will show signs of being ready for night-time training within a month of daytime dryness, whereas for others it may take from six to 12 months. All children are different and need to be treated as individuals, but so long as your child is ready for it, training can be a happy and rewarding experience for you both.

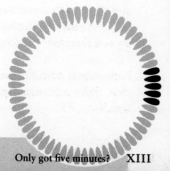

10 Only got ten minutes?

Most things in life benefit from good preparation and toilet training is no exception.

Your child will need to either have or be developing the following:

▶ Physical skills – being aware of the need to do a wee or poo and holding on to it for long enough to get to the potty or bathroom.
▶ Understanding – seeing how it all fits together.
▶ Communication skills – explaining what he needs.
▶ Self-help skills – being able to deal with clothing and hand-washing.

What can you as a parent do to help prepare your child in each of these areas?

Physical skills

(The ages given here can be defined as typical, but as in everything, children vary.)

Here are some things to try with a young baby:

▶ From an early age put your baby on the floor, babies need a firm surface to kick about on.
▶ The safest position for babies to sleep in is on their backs, but they still need to be allowed to play on their tummies, to strengthen their muscles. So remember – on his back to sleep and on his tummy to play.
▶ When holding your baby, as soon as he shows signs of being able to control his head, allow him to do so.

- ▶ Once your child is showing signs of being able to sit with support from cushions give him the opportunity to do so.
- ▶ Baby massage is a great way to enhance muscle tone.

At about a year old:

- ▶ Floor play is really important – your child needs a firm surface to push against to develop strength.
- ▶ Home safety becomes an issue. You need to make your home childproof to prevent accidents while also allowing your child to have the experiences he needs.
- ▶ Swimming is a great way to develop muscle tone and physical confidence.
- ▶ Think about joining a 'tumble tots' group.
- ▶ Don't forget your local park and playground.

At about 18 months:

- ▶ Take trips to local parks to experience the different play equipment.
- ▶ Encourage your child to walk when you go to the shops (holding your hand or wearing a safety harness).
- ▶ Teach your child to go up and down stairs safely.

From 18 months onwards allow your child a nappy-free period each day. Just before bath time is ideal. It is important that your child is allowed to have an accident so that he can experience wetness and can then make that connection between a wee and the potty.

By two years of age your child will be walking confidently and be able to squat with complete steadiness to play with an object on the floor. He will be becoming a keen climber and will be able to walk up and down stairs holding on to a hand rail. For toilet training a child needs to be able to squat and sit comfortably on a potty, and to be able to get himself up when finished.

Understanding

This is an essential skill for toilet training as your child needs to understand what is required of him.

To help the younger child:

▶ Talk to him about everything that you do – for example when changing his nappy explain to him why you are doing it.
▶ Role modelling is a great way to get the message across. He'll learn a lot by accompanying you and the rest of the family to the toilet.

By 18 months your child will explore his environment with increasing understanding. He will remember where an object is and will be beginning to follow a simple instruction. If you have given your child the opportunity to experience wetness he will be beginning to make the connection.

▶ Pretend play is perhaps one of the best ways to help your child to understand the world. This is the age to introduce a toy potty for his teddy or doll to sit on to begin to develop the understanding of what is expected.
▶ Encourage your child to be in the bathroom when his parents are using the toilet and let him see the sequence of events – including washing hands.
▶ This is an ideal time to introduce a book about toilet training for you both to share.

By two years of age your child will follow you around the house and imitate your domestic activities. He will engage in simple role play and substitute one item for another, e.g. he will pretend a brick is a car. He will follow simple instructions like 'go find your shoes' or 'put this in the bin'.

▶ Give your child lots of opportunities to make decisions that will help him understand what is going on around him.

Do this by giving him a choice between two things – for example, what colour socks he wants to wear or what he wants to drink.

▶ At this stage you should have a potty in the room that you use most. Let him know what it is for and if he wants to sit on it let him.

Communication

By 12 months your child will babble. He will understand certain words in their usual context, e.g. car, drink, cat. He may understand a simple instruction, e.g. 'give it to Daddy'. He may have a few recognizable words.

To help develop communication skills:

▶ Talk to your child. This is by far the best way to develop his speech.
▶ Repeat words. Children will understand far more than they can say. A child needs to hear a word many, many times before he will say it.
▶ Get into the habit of describing what you see, e.g. 'that's a big blue car' or 'look at the black cat'.
▶ Books are a fantastic way to develop speech and understanding.

By 18 months your toddler will chatter continually to himself while playing. Your child will have approximately between six and 20 recognizable words. He will also often repeat the last word said to him in a sentence. To help him:

▶ Repeat a word back to him when you hear him say it. This will encourage him to say it again.
▶ When your child has said a word add another word to it. For example, if your child said cat, say 'yes, black cat'. This is

teaching him that he is right, and also you are modelling to him how to put two words together to make longer sentences.

▶ Give your child choices wherever possible, but keep it simple and only offer two choices at a time. This will encourage him to talk to say which of the two he wants.

By two years of age children usually have about 50 recognizable words in their vocabulary but will understand many more. Your child will link two words together in a simple sentence and will constantly repeat words said to him. Remember to use lots of repetition of the words wee and poo and link them to the real thing.

Self-help skills

By the age of two children can usually assist with dressing and undressing, and can feed themselves competently with a spoon and drink from a feeder cup without difficulty. It is very important not to get stressed about any mess or mistakes your child makes, just let him try. Give your child plenty of opportunity to practice self-help skills, with lots of praise for any small success.

All of the above skills are essential to your child's development and to their chance of a short, successful potty training journey. By taking a holistic view of your child's skills, you will be helping to ensure a happy and stress-free toilet training experience for you both.

Introduction

If you have picked up this book, you may well be on the verge of toilet training your child and be looking for ways in which to tackle the process. Or perhaps you have a younger child who is not quite ready for toilet training and you are keen to find out the best way to prepare your child. Well, look no further, this book offers you a down-to-earth, sensible and sensitive approach to toilet training, which will be fun, enjoyable and quick.

The toilet training journey can be a deeply rewarding one, both for the parents and for the child. For the child it is reaching a milestone on the way to independence and an achievement that will boost her confidence and self-esteem. For the parents, it is the joy of seeing their child learning a new skill. It is also a turning point in reducing the workload and expense – NO MORE NAPPIES!

However, for many parents, if toilet training is not going well it can be a very frustrating time, and some dread the process. Perhaps they have an older child who encountered difficulties and they found toilet training a challenge, or they may have heard negative stories from other parents. Or they may just be feeling at a loss as to where to start. For the child, the toilet training process can become very anxiety provoking, especially if she does not have all the skills in place and is not really sure as to what is expected of her. By following the guidance and suggestions in this book, hopefully all of these feelings can be avoided.

At some stage in their development, the vast majority of children will become toilet trained. This is usually sooner rather than later but a few children – for a whole host of reasons that will be looked at in this book – will have delays and setbacks. The process can be simplified by accurately identifying when your child has acquired toilet readiness and by introducing a few simple measures that will prepare her for the journey. Working in partnership and allowing your child control of the process are key aspects. For a child, learning any new skill should be fun and enjoyable – not something to be dreaded.

Learning to use the potty or toilet isn't simply about sitting on it to do a wee or a poo; it encompasses a number of skills – including physical ones, self-help, understanding and communication. This book will outline the physical process that children need to go through and describe the skills that they need to acquire.

You will find a very useful 'Toilet readiness questionnaire' to help you identify if your child has acquired the skills to enable her to successfully navigate the toilet training journey. Don't worry if you find that your child has not got all the skills in place at this point – this book will not only help you to identify which areas of your child's development need to be fine-tuned, it will also help you with lots of fun suggestions for ways of helping her to acquire the skills needed.

This book recognizes that each child is an individual and that the toilet training process should be tailored to suit the needs of that individual. The journey should ideally be fun, quick and enjoyable. The emphasis is on the preparation. You will see the process described as a jigsaw puzzle. When all the pieces of the puzzle are in place and both you and your child are in the right frame of mind for toilet training (which is very important), the process will indeed prove to be fun, quick and enjoyable.

If you have met difficulties

For parents who have started the process and have met difficulties, this book has a number of real-life case studies that should help a lot. Although no two toilet training situations will be the same, many problematic toilet trainers share strikingly similar stories. It is hoped that these case studies will help you to feel that you are not alone. You may well identify with a case study and it will then offer you a detailed action plan to change the way in which you have been handling your child's toilet training. The way to change a child's behaviour, of course, is to change yours. Sometimes, when you are so closely involved in a situation, it is difficult to 'see the wood for the trees'. What these real-life case studies should offer to you is an insight into why the difficulty has occurred and a practical solution on how to turn the situation around.

Once you have read the first chapter, 'What is toilet training?', and then undertaken the 'Toilet readiness questionnaire' in Chapter 2, you should use the book as a manual. You will be able to refer to the clearly laid out chapters that address the needs of not only children just starting out on the toilet training journey, but also those who have encountered difficulties along the way. Once you have started on the toilet training journey, keeping the recommended diary will be of great benefit in enabling you to reflect on how the journey is progressing and perhaps resolving problems or adjusting your approach as you go along.

The toilet training journey isn't just about your child being clean and dry during the day, so we have also included a section on night-time training and, in addition, we examine the toileting issues that are important for your child when starting school.

For parents with children that have special needs – whether a physical disability or a learning disability – there is a chapter that offers further suggestions to deal with the particular situation in which you find yourself, and plenty of resources that you may find useful.

There are lots of special situations that may impact on toilet training so we have also included top tips for when your child is faced with one of those situations – for example, a new baby in the family, moving house or starting nursery or school.

So, to sum up, if your child is ready for toilet training and the process is undertaken with good preparation, you will be amazed at just how quickly your child will train. If your child has encountered difficulties, just a few simple changes to your management of the process may be all that is needed. This book offers you simple, down-to-earth suggestions to work in partnership with your child to reach the toilet training milestone in a relaxed, enjoyable manner. You can then, as a family, reap the rewards of 'NO MORE NAPPIES!'

1

What is toilet training?

In this chapter you will learn:
- *what toilet training is*
- *how toilet training has changed over the past generation*
- *what is the best age to start.*

Toilet training is simply the process of weaning your child out of nappies and teaching him how to use the potty or toilet when he passes urine (wee) and stools (poo). When your baby is first born he has no voluntary control over his bladder and bowel muscles. Over the months, as he grows, he will gradually develop control of these muscles and will reach the stage where he has enough control to begin to use a potty. Of course, although that is what happens, things are never quite that simple.

For a child to be able to successfully toilet train, he needs to have other skills in place in addition to the muscle control. Toilet training encompasses a whole host of skills; it also involves knowing when he needs to do a wee or poo and being able to communicate that to the person who is caring for him. It also means getting to the potty or toilet in time, being able to pull down his clothes and sitting on the potty. In addition, your child must be able to clean himself, pull his clothes back up and wash his hands when he's finished.

So, as you can see, a whole range of skills are involved, including: the **physical skills** of being aware of needing to do a wee or poo and holding on to it long enough to get to the potty; the **communication skills** to be able to explain what he needs to do;

the **self-help skills** of being able to deal with clothing and hand-washing; and of course the **understanding** of how it all fits together and a knowledge of the sequence of events.

It is useful to see it as a jigsaw puzzle and to think about how all the pieces need to fit together. In Chapter 2 we look in more detail at each piece of the puzzle and how it all does, in fact, fit together in a child who will successfully toilet train.

Insight

It is never too early to start sowing the seeds of what is expected of your child. Helping your child to prepare for learning this vital skill will ensure that the training goes smoothly. It helps to think of it like a jigsaw puzzle – helping your child to fit all the pieces together.

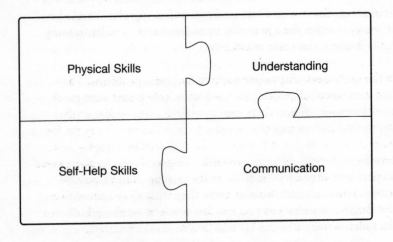

How has toilet training changed over the past generation?

A generation ago it was not uncommon for children to be out of nappies during the day by around their second birthday. Today the average age for a child to complete the process is more likely to be about two and a half to three years of age. In fact, if we go back further to your parent's day, the picture was very different again. Have you heard all those wonderful stories of babies that were out of nappies before they could walk? Very young babies were put on the potty at regular intervals during the day in the hope of catching something and this did often work, but, to be fair, this was toilet timing and not true toilet training.

So, why is it that children are training later than they were a generation ago? There is certainly no physiological reason for this change; it is more to do with the advances in technology and a change in our lifestyle than any physical changes in today's children. The first move towards later toilet training of our children coincided with the arrival of the automatic washing machine, which made the washing and drying of terry towelling nappies less labour-intensive so the incentive to get babies out of nappies was decreasing. But it was when the disposable nappy hit the market in the 1970s that the age of the commencement of toilet training really began to increase drastically.

In the early days, disposable nappies had their problems. The first versions of disposable nappies often leaked and were much more expensive to use than terry towelling nappies. But as they improved, their popularity increased and it became the norm for parents to use disposable nappies. Terry towelling nappies soon became to be seen as 'unfashionable'. Convenience has also played its part over the years – it is far easier to whip off a disposable nappy, replace it and throw it away than to have to deal with a wet, soggy, or soiled terry nappy that needs to be sluiced off into the toilet, soaked in a bucket and then washed and dried.

Also, during this same period the number of mothers working outside the home increased and we, as parents, embraced the convenience of disposable nappies. Further pressure was put upon time as both parents and children began to lead a much busier lifestyle than our parents did a generation ago. Childcare provision has also shaped our attitude to later toilet training. More and more children attend nurseries. They often start nursery at the age of two years and being in nappies is not an issue. A generation ago many children attended local playgroups where the policy was very clearly 'No nappies' and a child in nappies would be refused a place. Now, under the Disability Discrimination Act a child cannot be refused a place on the grounds of wearing a nappy, thereby removing another incentive to get children out of nappies early. All of these factors combined to change the toilet training situation.

Another important point to note, now that the use of disposable nappies is so widespread, is that these days many children never experience life without a nappy on until the day when toilet training starts. Over the years the improvements and advances in the manufacturing of disposable nappies have led us to a generation of babies and toddlers who have never felt wet or uncomfortable. Many children will start the toilet training process never having experienced the sensation of being 'wet'.

Insight

When changing your child's nappy, talk to him about what he has done, e.g. wet nappy – 'you've done a big wee, well done', or dirty nappy – 'you've done a lovely poo'. This way he will learn the words for wee and poo and it will make more sense when you start toilet training.

So, children are toilet training later and disposable nappies have certainly had their effect but what impact does all of this have for your child's toilet training journey? One thing you can do is to let your child experience wetness before you expect him to start the toilet training process. You can do this simply by letting him have a nappy-free period of time each day from the age of 18 months onwards. We have expanded on this idea in Chapters 2 and 3.

What works and what doesn't?

The aim of this book is to show you how and when to toilet train your child in a timely, pleasant and efficient way. We will look in greater detail at some of the *dos* and *don'ts* of the potty training process in later chapters, but here we can look briefly at some of the things that will work – and at some of the things that won't.

First, let's look at what you *shouldn't* do:

▶ *Don't start too soon – use our 'Toilet readiness questionnaire' in Chapter 2 to guide you. There is no magic age when every child will be ready for toilet training but you can certainly pinpoint when your child is ready. If you start too early for your child then you may cause the process to take longer than it needs.*

▶ *Don't get upset – there will always be accidents along the path to becoming clean and dry but you shouldn't let these upset you. Don't lose your temper, just clean up your child and get on with life. Also, don't let your feelings cause you to put pressure on your child – this could easily backfire.*

▶ *Don't let other people's opinions take over – do the questionnaire and be guided by your child and his abilities. It's important to note that the only person in control of toilet training is your child.*

Insight

All children are different and each child will train when he is ready. Do not feel pressurized by others to start training your child if you do not feel he is ready. This usually ends in disaster.

▶ *Don't start at the wrong time – any changes in routine may cause changes in your child's behaviour and, as we will see in Chapter 4, upsets and changes such as having a new baby in the family or going on holiday are not the time to start the toilet training process.*

Now, here's a bit about what does work:

▶ *Starting when your child is ready – use the 'Toilet readiness questionnaire' in Chapter 2.*
▶ *Being patient – your child will go at his own pace. Don't try to push your child to do more than he is ready for.*
▶ *Planning – choose the right time for you and your child (more in Chapters 2 and 4), get hold of the equipment you will need (see Chapter 3) and think about possible incentives.*

What age can you begin toilet training your child?

Good question! The answer is simple – when your child is ready! Most children will develop bladder and bowel control between the ages of two and three years of age. But remember, there is NO MAGICAL AGE as to when toilet training should start. There is no need to worry if your child does not appear ready and some of his friends have already started. All children are different; some will have the skills as young as 18 to 24 months but for others it may be nearer their third birthday. Both ends of the age range are fine. Don't forget that your child is an individual and he will become clean and dry with your help when you are both ready. Also, as we mentioned above, remember that even if your child has the skills in place, there are certain situations when it may be advisable to delay toilet training. There is more about these situations in later chapters. There can also be a wide variation within families as to the ages at which each child is trained. Also, don't forget, if you have a son, boys really do often train later than girls.

With the help of this book, you will be able to spot the clues when your child is ready. The 'Toilet readiness questionnaire' (Chapter 2) will identify which skills your child has in place and if he is ready to train. Again, don't worry if all those skills are not yet in place, there are lots of fun, easy to carry out suggestions on helping your child develop the skills needed when you have pinpointed which ones need attention. By following the many fun suggestions in this book, you will be able to prepare your child for the journey so that it is an enjoyable, stress-free one.

Case study: getting ready to toilet train

We used disposable nappies for Saskia from birth. I had toyed with the idea of using terry towelling nappies and had considered using disposables for the first few weeks and then moving to terry towelling after things had settled. But after a few weeks of sleepless nights, the thought of the extra work involved did not appeal and so we just carried on using disposables. Also, they were just so convenient. I was planning on going back to work when Saskia got to six months and I thought they would be easier to deal with at the child minder. At about 20 months I decided that we would get a potty and start leaving Saskia's nappy off in the evening for a while before her bath. I put the potty in the bathroom, which was close to the kitchen and just let Saskia wander around without a nappy. I started to talk to her about doing a wee in the potty and we read a children's book, *I Want My Potty*. A friend who had an older child also suggested that we did some pretend play with a toy potty and a teddy bear and Saskia really enjoyed this. After a couple of weeks I realized that Saskia was able to hold on to her wee for an hour or so but she still showed no interest in sitting on the potty. Then I started to take her nappy off a little earlier in the evening for about an hour and a half, she still did not have an accident. Then one evening when she was about 22 months, I was in the kitchen getting dinner ready when Saskia walked in and said she needed to do a wee. I casually said to her 'well you know where the potty is'. To my utter amazement a couple of minutes later she walked back into the kitchen with the potty to show me the wee she had done. This was the first time that she had ever sat on the potty, we continued like this until she turned two when I took a week off work and toilet trained her.

So what can we learn from this parent's experience? Let's look at the clues:

▶ *Saskia was able to hold on to her wee for at least an hour and a half, which demonstrated that she was acquiring bladder control.*

(Contd)

- *Saskia understood what the potty was for. It was interesting that she showed no interest in sitting on the potty until the time came when she needed a wee while she had her nappy off.*
- *Saskia had the communication skills to tell her mother that she needed a wee.*
- *Saskia had made the connection that when she felt the urge to do a wee, if she did not have a nappy on then she needed to go and sit on the potty.*

If we look back at the jigsaw puzzle that featured earlier on in this chapter, we can see that Saskia had all the skills in place: she knew what to do, how to do it and why she needed to do it. Her parents had also helped the process by allowing Saskia to experience life without a nappy, had explained to her what was expected and had reinforced that message by reading a children's book about toilet training to her. They had also not rushed Saskia to achieve dryness and had allowed all the pieces of the jigsaw puzzle to fall into place before starting the toilet training process in earnest. In fact, they had been very laid back and relaxed about the process. An important issue, which many parents overlook when toilet training their children, is that the only person who has true control over the situation is the child. You cannot force a child to do a wee or a poo in the potty if he decides that he does not want to. And as all parents know, if we let our children know just how much we want something then they are likely to decide that is just what they don't want.

Insight
Remember that toilet training should be fun and enjoyable for both child and adult.

Summary

In this first chapter we have had a brief look at just what toilet training is. We've seen the effect of the changes in society and in our attitude to toilet training over the last generation or so, and have outlined how we can decide the best time to start the toilet training journey. We've also looked at what works in toilet training and at some of the things that don't. Finally, we found many lessons to be learned in one parent's experience of the toilet training process so that we're now ready to take the next step.

In the next chapter we are going to look in detail at the skills that a child needs to be ready to start the journey. It is really important for your child that they have the skills in place for stress-free toilet training success. To assess if your child has those skills, there is the all-important 'Toilet readiness questionnaire' that we have talked about. This is a way of identifying where your child is at. But note that it is not a test, it is purely a way of seeing which skills your child has and of identifying any skills that may need to be fine-tuned. We also talk about working in partnership with your child, allowing your child to feel comfortable about sharing his control of the toileting experience with you. When children are put under pressure to toilet train, it often backfires. This is usually because the child feels that the control is being taken away from him and he will, of course, rebel against this. The next chapter also highlights when it is not a good time in a child's life to toilet train. Even when a child has all the skills in place, there may be situations when it is best to delay the training process.

10 THINGS TO REMEMBER

1 *For a child to be successfully toilet trained he needs to have gained a variety of skills – physical skills, communication skills, self-help skills and an understanding of what is expected. Remember it's a jigsaw puzzle; all the pieces need to fit together.*

2 *Children need to have experienced wetness before you can expect them to start the toilet training process. Begin to have a short nappy-free time each day from the age of 18 months onwards.*

3 *Don't start too soon. Your child does need to have the right skills in place.*

4 *Don't get upset if your child has an accident; remember he is learning a brand new skill.*

5 *Don't let other people's opinions take over, you know your child best.*

6 *Remember there are certain times in a child's life when it is best to delay training.*

7 *Be patient; if your child is ready to train it will all fall into place quickly.*

8 *Planning. Choose the right time for your child and make sure you have all the equipment in place that you will both need.*

9 *There really is no magical age to start. Most children will develop bladder and bowel control between the ages of two and three years.*

10 *Remember your child is an individual. He will do it when he is ready.*

2

Toilet readiness

In this chapter you will learn:
- *how to tell if your child is ready for toilet training*
- *how to use the 'Toilet readiness questionnaire'*
- *how to work in partnership with your child.*

What are the signs to look for?

As your child moves from being a baby to becoming a toddler, you will start to think about potty training and will need to know what to look out for so that you can decide the right time to start. There is no set time for this; there is a wide variation as to the age each individual child will toilet train, even within families. Remember that your child is an individual, so don't be worried if you find her other little friends are making progress but your child is not showing any interest. She will do it in her own good time when she has the skills and understanding in place. You cannot rush her development.

Insight
Girls often train earlier than boys.

This chapter will help you to decide if those skills are there and if it is the right time. Again, don't worry if it seems like your child is not ready; this chapter will also help to identify which areas could do with a helping hand. Then, in Chapter 3, there are lots of fun tips to help your child to develop the relevant skills.

Deciding if your child is ready can sometimes be quite bewildering. Any parent will tell you that they are often surprised at just how quickly their child is developing. At the age that children tend to toilet train (typically between the ages of two and three years), a child is learning and developing new skills every single day. Just think for a moment about the wide range of skills that we all have to acquire in just those first few short years – from the physical skills of learning to run, climb and jump, to the communication skills involved in making ourselves understood. This is such an exciting time for both parents and child, when every day is a new challenge with new experiences. Deciding if your child has the right skills in place to be toilet trained can be confusing and is a challenge in itself. So, how do you decide if your child is ready?

Toilet readiness is not just about being physically ready and being able to hold on to urine. As we said in Chapter 1, it is a bit like a jigsaw puzzle and you will need to have all the pieces in place before you start the toilet training journey. So, along with being physically ready, your child will need to understand the process and what is expected of her and also have the self-help and communication skills to enable her to do it. So let's look at the different types of skills needed.

1 Physical skills

During the first 18 months of life there is no real bowel or bladder control. Babies learn from their earliest days to empty their bowels or bladder when their tummies are full after a feed. This is simply a reflex action and they truly have no control over their muscles. Around 18 to 24 months this changes and some voluntary control begins to take over. But this is a slow process and it may still be some time before a child becomes aware that she needs to do a wee before the event rather than after. This table will show you the different phases of gaining control over bladder and bowels:

0–18 months	**Phase 1** No control over bladder/bowel.
18–24 months	**Phase 2** Beginning to develop some control. She will start to become aware after the wee or poo has happened.
24 months onwards	**Phase 3** Control increases and she becomes aware as the wee or poo is happening. **Phase 4** Control increases and she is aware just before the impending wee or poo. **Phase 5** She has the awareness and is able to hold on to the wee or poo long enough to get to the potty or the toilet. She can go for one and a half to two hours between each wee.

She is not physically ready until she has mastered Phase 5. There is nothing that you as a parent can do to speed up the process. It is a physical milestone that she will reach in her own good time. But, what you can do as a parent to help is to allow your child to experience wetness. This may sound surprising but, as we said before, because of the amazing disposable nappies that we now have, children often reach the age when toilet training becomes possible without ever having experienced the sensation of wetness. This can be quite a frightening feeling for them as it is so different from the feeling of weeing in a nappy and, in some cases, may well delay training, as a child needs to get over their fear of letting go. The easiest way to promote this is, from about 18 months of age, to allow your child to go without a nappy for a short period each day – a good time is before a bath. If your child has an accident while she is not wearing a nappy, just clean it up. All children have accidents – it is normal and just part of the process – but it can be helpful to say to your child 'That's a wee, Mummy and Daddy do that in the toilet and you can do it in the potty'. Also, allowing your child to have the odd accident like this will help her to make sense of what is expected of her and to realize what a wee feels like.

So, although you cannot speed up the time it takes for your child to reach Phase 5, you can, while you are waiting and watching, improve your child's skills and understanding. In this way you will ensure that when the time comes for toilet training, she is fully equipped and the process will be made easier.

Parent's comment – looking for clues

I began to notice that Emily (two years and four months) would sometimes sit or stand still and stop playing for a few minutes – she seemed to be concentrating. It took me a few days to realize that she was a doing a wee. About two weeks after I first noticed this she started to pull at her nappy and ask for a new one. We started to toilet train her at this stage and a month or so later she was dry and clean during the day. I think it really helped that we took our clues from her.

Start to look for these physical clues and spend some time observing your child for the following telltale signs:

1 *She is able to hold on to wee for about one and a half to two hours.*

2 *She has a dry nappy after her daytime nap.*
3 *She will sit or stand still for a while when doing a wee or a poo in her nappy.*
4 *She makes a grunting noise when doing a poo in her nappy.*
5 *She will squat when doing a poo in a nappy.*
6 *She will show discomfort at a soiled or wet nappy.*

Your child may not show all of these physical signs, just some of them. She may also begin to ask for a new nappy.

---

2 Self-help skills

Self-help skills are about your child developing the ability to do things for herself. So, for example, being able to feed herself is a self-help skill. It is also a sign that she is beginning to understand and make sense of the world around her. As she starts to play her part in the world, she will start to imitate what she sees around her and will engage in pretend play, such as putting teddy to bed or giving teddy a drink. So, what self-help skills does your child need in order to be able to toilet train successfully? Look for the following:

1 *She is able to sit quietly for a few minutes engaged in an activity.*
2 *She will potter off and play on her own for a short time without adult help.*
3 *She may attempt to take off her nappy if it is wet or soiled.*
4 *She will try to undress – for example, attempting to pull down her trousers.*
5 *She will take an interest in other family members' toileting habits.*

Insight
Encourage your child to help dress and undress herself as soon as she shows an interest. Try making it into a game or a challenge.

From the age of about 22 months, Tom was fascinated by what happened in the toilet. He would follow whoever went in there and watch what happened. It became a bit embarrassing, as some of our friends (understandably) did not fancy a toddler watching them. So we had to be clear with him as to whom he could accompany. Anyway, he seemed to pick up very quickly what was expected of him and he trained much more quickly than his older brother had done. I am sure it was helped by the fact that he understood the process of doing a wee or a poo and flushing the toilet. In fact he never used the potty and went straight to the toilet.

Insight

As soon as you can, encourage your child to sit down and to concentrate on a short activity. This will make it easier when she needs to sit on the potty.

3 Understanding

Understanding plays a huge part in the toilet training process and the importance of a child understanding what is expected of her is often overlooked. Imagine you were starting a new job and you had been given the job because you had shown that you had the skills to do the job. But if you had never done this particular type of work before, it would be quite reasonable to expect to be shown how to do the job a number of times before you got it right. Well, it is no different with toilet training.

Your child needs to understand the process and what is expected of her. From the age of about 18 months onwards children will begin to follow simple commands or instructions. For example, 'please close the door' or 'can you get your shoes?'. Understanding is an important part of potty training and in deciding whether your child is ready. Children need to be able to follow a simple instruction and to be able to understand what is expected of them when you ask them if they need to sit on the potty to do a wee or a poo.

Parent's comment – making sense of it all

I found a great book in the library called *I Want my Potty*. Kelsey (two years and five months) loved the book and I really think it helped her make sense of what toilet training was all about, plus the fact she wanted to be like the little princess in the book and sit on the potty.

4 Communication

Around the age of two years, children are rapidly developing their communication skills and are beginning to link two words together, i.e. me drink, daddy home. At this stage it is helpful for a child if she has words that she can use to communicate with you that she needs a wee or a poo. You can help in this area by giving her the words she needs from an early age. When you are changing her nappy or going to the toilet yourself, use these words so that she will make the connections. Different families use different words for these bodily functions but it doesn't really matter what words you use – so long as you and your child understand their meanings.

Communication is not just about spoken language, of course, it is also about gestures and for some children who perhaps have a limited vocabulary, pointing may be their way of getting the message across. Look out for this and for other gestures your child may use.

Understanding and communication go hand in hand. So, a child needs to understand a situation before she is able to communicate about the situation.

> **Insight**
> Let your child spend time in the bathroom with you and talk to her about what you are doing on the toilet.

How to tell if your child is ready

We have now looked at the signs of toilet readiness and you need to remember that it's a bit like a jigsaw puzzle – your child needs to have all the pieces in place for successful toilet training:

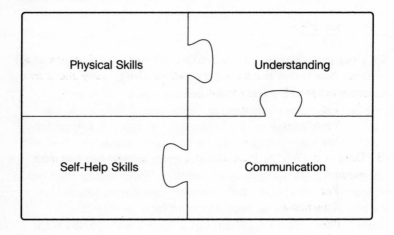

Physical Skills

Understanding

Self-Help Skills

Communication

Now spend some time thinking about the skills required and observe your child. You may well be amazed at what she can do. Then fill out the 'Toilet readiness questionnaire' that follows. It is a good idea, if possible, to do this with your partner. Or, if your child is at a nursery or with a childminder or nanny, you may find it helpful to do it with them too.

Toilet readiness questionnaire

Go through all the questions, adding up the appropriate score for each question. Remember that this is not a test or a competition, it is purely a way of assessing where your child is at and if there are any skills that you may need to help your child to develop.

PHYSICAL SIGNS

1 *Does your child have dry periods of approximately one and a half to two hours during the day?*

Yes	2
Sometimes	1
No	0

2 *Does your child pass a fair amount of urine in their nappy at a time (you will notice the nappy feels suddenly heavy and warm from the freshly passed urine)?*

Yes	2
Sometimes	1
No	0

3 *Does your child go quiet and still when passing urine in their nappy?*

Yes	2
Sometimes	1
No	0

4 Does your child ever wake up from a daytime nap with a dry nappy?

     Yes   2

     Sometimes   1

     No   0

5 Does your child have regular well-formed bowel movements at relatively predictable times during the day?

     Yes   2

     Sometimes   1

     No   0

6 Does your child give a physical or verbal sign when having a bowel movement? For example, a grunt or squatting or coming to tell you?

     Yes   2

     Sometimes   1

     No   0

7 Does your child dislike wearing a wet or dirty nappy?

     Yes   2

     Sometimes   1

     No   0

SELF-HELP SIGNS

8 Can your child sit quietly in one position for between two and five minutes while undertaking an activity?

     Yes   2

     Sometimes   1

     No   0

9 Does your child show an interest in other people's bathroom habits? For example, do they want to watch you use the toilet?

     Yes   2

     Sometimes   1

     No   0

10 Is your child at a generally co-operative stage for learning a new skill?

     Yes   2

     Sometimes   1

     No   0

UNDERSTANDING AND COMMUNICATION

11 *Can your child follow a simple instruction? For example, 'go and get your shoes'.*

        Yes   2

        Sometimes   1

        No   0

12 *Can your child understand the concept of putting something into a container? For example, 'go and put the bag in the bin'.*

        Yes   2

        Sometimes   1

        No   0

13 *Does your child have words or signs for urine and stool?*

        Yes   2

        Sometimes   1

        No   0

SCORING

Now check your total score as follows to find out if your child is ready for potty training:

0 to 12 points
Your child does not have toilet readiness yet. Use the questionnaire to help you decide which areas you need to help your child to develop skills in. For example, if your answer to Question 13 was 'No' then you will need to work on your child's communication skills, so go to Chapter 3 where you will find lots of fun and easy-to-do suggestions to help your child develop the skills needed.

Leave it for a month and then complete the questionnaire again. Don't worry at all if you find that they are still not ready – remember all children are individuals and will get there in their own good time, with your help. Continue to help your child develop the skills that she needs and use the questionnaire as a means to assess her progress.

13 to 18 points

Your child is showing signs of toilet readiness. Look again at the questions where your child has scored a 1 or a 0, then go to Chapter 3 on preparation for toilet readiness and look at the fun suggestions for developing those skills. When you feel your child is ready, read the section below on 'Working in partnership with your child', then turn to Chapters 4 and 5 and begin the journey.

19 to 26 points

Your child has all the skills in place. Read the section below on 'Working in partnership with your child', then turn to Chapters 4 and 5 and begin the journey.

Insight

Use the questionnaire as your guide to whether your child is ready or needs a helping hand. It really is important that she has all the skills in place for toilet training to be a success, so don't rush her if she is not quite ready. Rushing at this stage may prolong the training.

Working in partnership with your child

Believe it or not, the only person who has control when it comes to toilet training is your child. You cannot make a child do a wee or a poo in the potty if she decides that she doesn't want to. For this simple reason, working in partnership with your child plays a huge part in toilet training.

Your child needs to feel secure and comfortable about letting go. If your child begins to feel that doing a wee or a poo is very important to her parent or caregiver then she may begin to feel that control is being taken away from her. This may well have a negative impact and she may decide that she does not want to co-operate. Before you start to toilet train, it is a good idea to think about your child's personality and assess just how receptive she is to learning a new skill. If you have a child who is generally co-operative and easygoing, she is more likely just to get on with toilet training. However, given that most children train around the ages of two to three years and that this is also the age when temper tantrums are most common, you may well need to think about some incentives for your child. In Chapter 3 you will find a section on star charts, which can be a fun, useful incentive to use for the reluctant or unco-operative child.

Insight

It's a good idea – for all sorts of reasons – to read to your child from an early age. But one particular benefit it will bring is that it will make introducing a book on toilet training seem like a natural thing to do.

Parent's comment – watching your own behaviour

Lily (aged two years and five months) was becoming a nightmare to train. We had been at it for about three weeks when it was clear that both our tempers were flaring out of control. To start with she had been quite good with only the odd accident each day, but then I started to get cross with her, which just made her worse. My mother came to stay for a week and, after a very fraught day of accidents, I broke down in tears. My mother started to laugh, which of course made me even crosser. She said 'But can you not see, you are both so alike? Each of you wants control, and the other won't let you have it.' It was a real eye-opener and I realized that the only way Lily was going to change her behaviour was for me to change mine. So the following morning, instead of getting cross when she had an accident, I just cleaned it up

(Contd)

without a comment, then when Lily was successful I gave her lots of praise. By the time my mother left at the end of the week, Lily was almost dry. Thank goodness for mothers.

Although, generally speaking, you should start the toilet training process when you find that your child is ready, there are certain times in a child or parent's life when it is not a good time to toilet train. Any effort that either you or your child may put in at these times may well be wasted, so be sure to pick your time carefully. Listed below are situations when it is probably best to avoid starting the toilet training process:

1 *If your child is going through a negative phase – these don't usually last very long so wait for it to pass and then consider starting the toilet training process.*
2 *If the child or parent is unwell – if your child is unwell it could easily affect her bowels or bladder or could just make her 'out of sorts' so that she cannot do her best. Similarly, if you are not on top form, you will not have the patience necessary to do the best by your child.*
3 *If there is a new baby in the family – this can be very distracting for both child and parent. You will be tired and your child may be feeling left out.*
4 *If your child is starting nursery or playgroup – going to a new nursery or playgroup is enough of a change for a toddler to cope with, so don't give her even more to think about.*
5 *If there is a change of childcare – again, this will involve huge changes for your child.*
6 *If you are taking a holiday away from home – although holidays are usually enjoyable, they still involve major changes in routine that will make toilet training very difficult.*
7 *If you are moving house – get your routine sorted out when you are settled in your new home and then consider starting potty training.*

8 *During a major family upset – if you're upset, or routines are changed, then it will not be a good time to start toilet training.*

Working parents

If you are a working parent, even imagining how you are going to toilet train your child can be very difficult, especially if you are out at work full-time. Despite the possibly more difficult circumstances, there are various options available to you. You need to decide which option is going to work for you and your child, taking into consideration the type of childcare that you are using. Let's look at the options available to working parents and some comments made by parents in these circumstances:

TOILET TRAIN YOUR CHILD YOURSELF

For example, taking annual leave for a period of time.

Parent's comments

I decided that Saskia (two years old) was showing all the signs that she was ready to be toilet trained. I was working three days a week and she went to a local childminder who was very experienced, but I decided that I wanted to train her at home myself. I took a week off work and I planned a very quiet week just pottering about at home in the mornings and going out for a short period in the afternoon. We were lucky, it all fell into place – we had a relaxing week and by the time she went back to Fay, the childminder, the following week, she was out of nappies.

USE A JOINT APPROACH

For example, toilet training at home and in the childcare setting at the same time:

Parent's comments

I was very nervous at the prospect of toilet training Joshua (two years and nine months) and had been putting it off. We had a nanny, as I was working full time. The nanny asked me one day if I had any plans to train him and I expressed my anxieties. We sat down together and discussed a plan of action with a star chart suggested by the nanny. She started the whole thing off and we followed her guidance in the mornings, evenings and weekends when we were with him. It was all quite painless really. I don't know why I was so worked up about it all.

LEAVE THE TRAINING TO THE CHILDCARE SETTING

Parent's comments

I had not given much thought to toilet training Millie (two years and six months), who was at nursery full time. Then one weekend we were at a friend's house who had an older child who was using the potty. I was in the bathroom changing Millie's nappy when she suddenly announced that she wanted to do a wee on the potty. I was speechless with surprise when she did, in fact, do a wee. On the following Monday when I took her into nursery, I spoke to one of the nursery staff. They said that she had been showing a lot of interest in watching the older children using the potty. They said that they would start to ask Millie if she wanted to use the potty.

Nurseries and childcare

Having seen some of the ways that working parents can manage the toilet training process, let's look at some of the advantages that childcare brings to this time in your child's life. Being in a childcare situation can have many benefits when it comes to toilet training. One of the most important benefits of childcare has to be that of being in a peer group. Children love to imitate, especially what their friends or slightly older children are doing, and they will be quite likely to model their behaviour on their peers. Watching some other little person using the potty is the ideal way of understanding what is expected of you.

Secondly, nurseries often have child-size toilets, which are fantastic for making the children feel safe. As we saw previously, children need to feel comfortable about letting go and anything – such as child-size toilets – that can help them feel this way will obviously be helpful.

A third point to note is that if your child is at nursery they will be allocated a key worker whose responsibility it is to monitor your child's progress and development, and they will be actively involved in any decisions about toilet training. For a parent, having someone to discuss things with can be especially useful at the potty training stage. One of the major benefits of using childcare is that the staff will have had lots of experience and so will have a clear view as to whether your child is ready and will, more likely than not, be quite relaxed about toileting.

Nurseries will have clear policies and procedures around toilet training and will have routines in place so, for example, the children will be encouraged to go to the toilet before morning snack, before lunch and before nap times. Children love routines, and again they help children to make sense of the world around them and to understand what is expected of them.

One important thing to note is that there needs to be clear communication between parents and carers. Some nurseries have a communication book for each child so that the parents can see what type of day their child has had. So information about sleeps or naps, what your child ate for lunch, etc. can be recorded for you to read. Progress around toilet training can also be recorded in this way. It can be extremely helpful to arrange a meeting with your child's key worker to discuss if your child is ready. As suggested earlier, it may be useful to look at the 'Toilet readiness questionnaire' together (see above). Discuss the nursery's policy and their way of managing toilet training. You will be able to work out how you can do it in partnership, remembering that your child needs a consistent approach.

Case study: two failed attempts at toilet training

Phillip (two years and eight months) was the first child in the family. His younger sibling had been born when he was 19 months old. His mother was at home, full-time caring for both children. His father was working long hours and was only really around at weekends.

The problem
Phillip's parents had tried on two occasions to toilet train him. The first time, when he was two years old, was not long after the birth of his sibling and the second occasion was when he was two years and four months. On both occasions it had ended in tantrums and lots of accidents. Both parents had found the whole situation exasperating and were dreading the thought of another attempt! Phillip was due to start playgroup when he reached three years old in just a few months' time and the playgroup was keen for him not to be in nappies. Phillip was a very busy child with a short attention span and he tended to flit from one activity to another. At the previous attempts at toilet training he had been very reluctant to sit on the potty. However, he had good bladder control and did a poo in his nappy every morning after breakfast. He also had a clear understanding of what he needed to do – it was just that he was not keen to co-operate.

The reason
The two previous attempts had failed and Phillip's parents had become quite cross with him during the training. There was also a younger child to care for, so often Phillip's mother had been busy feeding or changing the baby when Phillip needed to use the potty. Phillip also was a very busy child who had a short attention span and got easily bored, so he was reluctant to sit on the potty.

The solution
There were a number of steps that Phillip's parents needed to take to ensure that their next attempt at potty training was successful:

1 *Help him to develop his concentration span and to complete an activity rather than to flit from one activity to another.*
2 *Help him to learn to sit on the potty.*
3 *Find a way to reward Phillip that would appeal to him.*

The plan
To achieve their goal, Phillip's parents followed a carefully developed plan:

WEEK ONE
Days 1, 2 and 3
- *Three times a day, Phillip was encouraged to sit at the table with his mother and undertake an activity for three minutes.*
- *These activities were varied so that Phillip did not get bored.*
- *He was given the choice of two activities each time so that he felt that he had ownership of the activities. It gave him a feeling of being in control. The activities varied from drawing, sticking, looking at a book together, building Lego and playing a matching game.*
- *A star chart was introduced. Every time Phillip sat for three minutes he was rewarded with a sticker, with the promise of a small treat when he had accumulated six stickers.*

Days 4 and 5
- *The length of time for each activity was increased to five minutes, three times a day.*

(Contd)

- One of the choices now included pretend play with a teddy and toy potty.
- The star chart continued.

INTERIM PROGRESS REPORT

Phillip was now happily sitting down with his mother three times a day and would concentrate well for at least five minutes each time. On some occasions it was longer than this, so his concentration skills were steadily being improved. The star chart had been a great success and Phillip was beginning to ask if he could do an activity so that he could put a sticker on the star chart.

Days 6 and 7
- *The length of each activity was extended to eight minutes.*

WEEK TWO
Days 1, 2 and 3
- *Phillip was encouraged to sit on the potty before each of the three play times.*
- *Sitting on the potty was added to the star chart. So Phillip was rewarded with a sticker for sitting on the potty and another one for undertaking an activity.*

INTERIM PROGRESS REPORT

On Day 4 of the second week, Phillip had his first successful wee in the potty. To his delight he was given two stickers. On Day 7 of the second week he announced that he did not want to wear nappies anymore and, apart from the odd accident, by the end of Week three he was clean and dry. Alongside his success with potty training, he had also improved his concentration span dramatically and this would, of course, prove to be of great benefit to him when he started playgroup.

The outcome
Phillip had the physical ability, understanding and communication skills in place. He had needed to develop the self-help skill of being

able to concentrate for a short period of time and to accept the idea of sitting on the potty. This was done in a very gradual way with lots of fun activities and rewards. The parents worked in partnership with Phillip by giving him the chance to choose which activity he undertook.

Conclusion
The first time Phillip's parents had tried to toilet train him was shortly after the birth of his younger sibling. This is never really a good time as everyone is tired and small babies need a lot of attention.

In Phillip's case, he needed a parent who was able to spend time developing his concentration skills and was able to give him the attention that he needed at the time. This was much easier to do when his sibling was a bit older.

Summary

In this chapter we have looked at how the pieces of the jigsaw puzzle fit into place and the type of skills that your child needs. The 'Toilet readiness questionnaire' should have helped you to decide if your child is ready. Don't worry if she has not yet mastered all the skills needed. It is very important to remember that all children are different and they all get there in their own good time. In the next chapter you will find lots of easy-to-do suggestions to help your child to successfully develop any skills needed.

10 THINGS TO REMEMBER

1 *Remember that all children are individuals. There's no set age for toilet training, even within families.*

2 *Don't forget that girls often – but not always – train earlier than boys.*

3 *To be ready to start toilet training your child needs to have the awareness and be able to hold on to her wee or poo long enough to get to the potty or the toilet. She needs to be able to go one and a half to two hours between each pee.*

4 *Remember again, it's important for children to experience wetness before you start toilet training so let them have a nappy-free period every day from 18 months.*

5 *To be ready for toilet training your child needs to be able to sit for a few minutes and concentrate.*

6 *Children need to understand what's expected of them, so encourage your child to follow simple instructions such as 'find your shoes', 'put this in the bin' and 'close the door'.*

7 *It is helpful if children are able to communicate when they need to go to the toilet, so teach them the words wee and poo – or whatever words you use in your family.*

8 *Don't forget to complete the 'Toilet readiness questionnaire'.*

9 *Once you have done the questionnaire, use the outcome as a guide to the next stage for your child.*

10 *Remember to work in partnership with your child. The only person that has control over training is your child.*

3

Preparation for toilet readiness

In this chapter you will learn:
* *about the equipment you may find useful*
* *how to develop the skills your child needs for successful potty training*
* *some incentives you might like to use.*

So, you have filled out the 'Toilet readiness questionnaire' in Chapter 2 and maybe you have found that there are certain areas or skills that your child needs help to develop or fine-tune. Or, you are just beginning to think about toilet training and you are keen to have all the parts of the jigsaw puzzle in place before you tackle the project. Well, this chapter will help you and your child to complete the puzzle.

This chapter is about getting prepared. It is full of information about the type of equipment that you may find useful during the potty training process. It then goes on to look at how you can develop the skills essential to toilet training that we talked about in Chapter 2, and also gives some suggestions about the sort of incentives you might want to use with your child and when and how to use them.

There's plenty of advice about the preparation necessary and how you can help your child but, above all, you should remember that the process of getting your child ready for toilet training should be fun, enjoyable and light-hearted.

A word about wearing nappies

Before we go on to examine the sorts of things that you will be using in your quest to get your child out of nappies, let's look at the nappies themselves. The disposable nappies that we have on the market nowadays are really quite magical. They not only absorb huge amounts of urine, but they also keep children amazingly dry and comfortable. As we said previously, many children have never experienced the true sensation of wetness before they start the toilet training process. Also, due to convenience, we tend to pop a nappy straight back on after changing a dirty one. Our children today are therefore almost always comfortable in their soft, dry, padded nappies. But the main aim of potty training is to do away with nappies, so getting them out of their nappies must be a focus for the main part of the whole process.

Remember that it must feel very strange for some children to suddenly be expected not to wear a nappy. We have taken them out of their comfort zone with all that lovely soft padding gone at just the point when we want them to feel at ease and ready to learn new things. So, what can you do to help ease the transition from nappy to no more nappies?

It might sound strange, but do allow your child to experience what true wetness is. Remember, we touched on this briefly in Chapter 2. From the age of about 18 months, let him have a short, nappy-free period every day. An ideal time is before a bath, so that if he does have an accident he will soon be having a bath anyway. For the first week, leave him for ten minutes without a nappy and gradually increase by ten minutes each week, until he is happy to go without a nappy for an hour or so.

Going without a nappy will confer two benefits:

1 *Awareness of what it feels like to be wet. The odd accident is useful so that your child can see and feel the wee.*
2 *Getting your child used to not wearing a nappy. Soon he will be wearing pants and the nappies will have gone for good,*

so it is a great idea to introduce this feeling to him in the preparation period.

Insight

Remember to start the nappy-free time before you start toilet training to encourage an awareness of wetness.

Now let's look at some of the items – pants, appropriate clothing, potties and so on – that you might want to get hold of in preparation for the toilet training process.

Pull-ups versus pants

Once you have decided to toilet train your child you need to make the decision as to whether you use pants or pull-ups (disposable) – or some parents decide to use a combination of both. Let's look at the pros and cons for each.

The advantages *Pants*	*Pull-ups*
Quick and easy to pull up and down.	Easy to dispose of if your child has an accident.
You can choose your child's favourite colour or character.	No extra washing.
You child will understand what it feels like to be wet if he has an accident.	No extra mess if your child soils the pull-up.

The disadvantages *Pants*	*Pull-ups*
Extra washing.	Expensive.
Having to deal with soiled pants.	Some children will treat them as nappies. Will not help to develop an awareness of wetness.

Whichever you decide to use after looking at the list of pros and cons, if you find one is not working then you can always swap to the other.

Parent's comments

A friend recommended pull-ups and I did buy a pack when we first started to train Bibi. But I found them a complete waste of money as Bibi just used them like she would a nappy.

Mother of Bibi, aged two years and eight months

I used pull-ups really successfully and it saved on extra washing and scraping poo off pants, which I really did not want to do!

Mother of Ahmed, aged two years and six months

Insight
Two points to note about pants

1 *It is well worth taking your child with you on your shopping trip and letting him choose which pants he would like. It gives children a real sense of ownership and control if they are allowed to choose which pants to buy and it will make your child feel important and grown-up.*
2 *When buying pants, always get the next size up – it makes it much easier for your child to pull his pants up and down if they are slightly loose rather than fitting too snugly.*

Clothes

In the early days of toilet training, when your child may not have very much time between feeling the urge to go to the toilet and it actually happening, it is best to keep clothing simple and, when indoors, to keep it to the minimum. So, when indoors, a T-shirt and pants or pull-ups are all that is needed. For when you are going out without a nappy, simple clothing is best. This will ensure fewer accidents and that your child will not panic that they won't get on the potty in time. Let's look at what would be suitable:

Ideal clothing
▶ *Trousers or shorts with an elasticated waistband.*
▶ *Dresses or skirts – not tight around the knees or too voluminous.*

Avoid
▶ *Dungarees.*
▶ *Trousers or shorts with buttons or zips.*
▶ *Any clothing with poppers.*
▶ *Tights.*
▶ *Tight dresses or skirts.*

Insight
Don't let your child wear his best clothes when training in case they get soiled.

Parent's comments

Jack toilet trained during the summer and we were lucky that we had floorboards and no carpets downstairs, so we

(Contd)

just let him run around with a T-shirt on. In the early days we didn't even bother with pants.

Father of Jack, aged three years

The first couple of times that we went out without nappies, Jessica had an accident because she could not get her tights down in time. I learnt quickly from that mistake and she wore loose, elastic-waist trousers after that. She found them much easier to pull down.

Mother of Jessica, aged two years and three months

Equipment

Having looked at the pants or pull-ups that you will use instead of nappies, and at the suitable clothing that you will have to consider to make your potty training path as smooth as possible, we will now look at the items of equipment you may need.

Insight

If your child is really not keen on using a potty, try him on the toilet instead and bypass the potty if need be.

THE POTTY

The most important item has to be the potty. Again, it will help if you can take your child shopping with you if you are going to buy a new one. Let him choose which colour he would like. It is useful to have two potties, one for the bathroom and the other for whichever room your child spends a lot of time in. If you are going to buy two, it is a very good idea to get them both the same colour. You wouldn't be the first parent caught out by a child who decides they want to do a wee in the blue one upstairs rather than the red one downstairs.

You don't need to buy the all-dancing, musical, light-flashing potty. A plain, wide-based, sturdy potty is just as good – and much cheaper.

....

Insight

Buy two potties the same colour. One for the bathroom and the other for the room that your child will spend most time in during the day.

....

A CHILD'S TOILET SEAT

Some children choose never to use a potty or, for some, the potty will be short-lived and they will move on to using the toilet quite quickly. It is a very good idea to purchase a child's toilet seat for your child. Sitting on a grown up toilet can be a very frightening experience for children. They may feel like they are going to fall down the toilet, so having a child-sized toilet seat will ease the transition until they are physically a bit bigger and also have the confidence to use an adult toilet without one. Child toilet seats attach easily to the toilet and will offer your child a sense of security when using the toilet. There are many different types on the market to choose from.

STEPS

Having a little step in the bathroom is a great idea for three reasons:

1 *Your child can use it to help him climb onto the toilet.*
2 *When sitting on the toilet he can rest his feet on the step. When doing a poo your child's feet should be against a firm surface with knees bent, rather than dangling in mid-air. This helps him to empty his bowels fully and is particularly important if he ever suffers from constipation.*
3 *Your child can also use the step to stand on when using the sink to wash his hands or clean his teeth.*

Most baby and children's equipment shops will offer a selection of steps suitable for use by your toddler in the bathroom. They are usually made of a sturdy plastic and come in a variety of colours.

What you may need for getting out and about

Going out with a child who has just toilet-trained can be a daunting prospect. Accidents are always possible, so some preparation is necessary to make sure that you and your child don't get 'caught short'. Of course, you need to take spare clothes and pants to start with, but what about if he suddenly decides he needs to go to the toilet and you don't feel comfortable about him using the public toilets or he feels uncomfortable sitting on an adult toilet? As always, manufacturers have come up with solutions to sell to us. You can now buy foldable potties that have a plastic disposable liner inside. You simply unfold the potty to create a robust, standard-size potty. When your child has done a wee or a poo, you tie up the liner and dispose of it, then the potty folds flat for easy transportation again. If your child is used to using a toilet instead of a potty, you can also purchase collapsible child-size toilet seats that you can fold up and put in your bag.

Parents often worry about their child having an accident in the buggy or car seat. A perfect way to protect these surfaces is to use a change mat that many of the nappy manufacturers make. These are absorbent disposable mats that have a plastic covering. They can be used to protect the buggy or car seat in the early days of toilet training or if you have a long car journey. They will give you extra protection and peace of mind in case of an emergency.

Skills

Now that we've looked at some of the practical things you will have to think about in preparation for toilet training, let's go on to look at how you can develop the skills that your child needs before you begin toilet training. By now you will have done the 'Toilet readiness questionnaire' in Chapter 2, so you will be aware which skills your child has already achieved and which ones he may need help in developing. Here's some guidance about each of the skills required:

1 PHYSICAL SKILLS

As we have already discussed, you cannot do anything to make your child physically able to hold on to urine – that will only happen when his muscles develop the necessary control.

However, the one physical skill that you can encourage your child with at this stage is that of developing independence around getting dressed and undressed. Toilet training is not just about being able to wee or poo in a potty, it is also about being able to pull your pants and trousers down in time and then pull them back up with confidence.

Insight

Encourage your child to develop independence skills as soon as he is ready, e.g. helping to dress and undress himself.

A great technique for helping your child learn to dress and undress himself is 'backward dressing'. For example, if you want him to learn how to put on his socks, first put his socks on for him, but don't pull the sock up from the ankle. Then take your child's hands and guide him to pull his socks up from the ankle. Do this each morning until he is able to pull up his own socks from the ankle. Next, put his socks on but do not pull them over the heel. Again take your child's hands and guide the socks over the heel and then let him finish off the job of pulling the socks up from the ankle. Once your child is used to pulling them over the heel then just pull the socks on over the toes and guide your child's hands. Very soon he will be able to put his socks on with little or no help.

Do the same with trousers. Pull the trousers up to your child's hips, then take his hands and guide them up to the waist. The next step is to pull them up to the knees and help guide your child and so on until his trousers are up.

Do this with all items of clothing and you will be surprised at just how quickly he learns to dress himself. It is exactly the same with undressing – don't forget it is easier to take clothes off than put them on.

So, in just the same way as with dressing, if you're teaching your child to undress, start with taking off socks. Pull the socks down over the heel and then guide your child's hands to pull the sock off completely.

Allowing your child to take charge of dressing and undressing himself can be a great boost to his self-confidence.

2 SELF-HELP SKILLS

One skill that will truly help your child to successfully toilet train is the ability to sit for a few minutes and concentrate. Some children find this easier than others, but all children can be encouraged to develop their concentration span. Below is a list of suggestions for activities that you can do with your child to develop and extend his concentration span. It is best to start with little and often, so maybe try three short sessions a day for two to three minutes to start with. Ideally it needs to be done away from distraction, i.e. TV and radio off, and a clear space with no other distractions around.

This is a list of suggestions; you may have others of your own that your child is particularly interested in. You do not need to do all the activities – just choose the ones your child is interested in. Remember it is about having fun in addition to developing concentration. Also, don't forget to praise your child for playing so well. It is always a good idea to give him a choice of two activities to do – as we said before, it allows your child to feel he has control over what he is doing. As his concentration span gradually increases, gently encourage him to complete the activity rather than stopping after the required amount of time, for example, by finishing the jigsaw puzzle or completing the matching game.

Timetable in sessions during the day when your child has an opportunity for quiet play on his own or with you. Children love playing games, whether it is an imaginary game or a sit down with mum and dad game.

Activities to develop concentration

- *Sharing a book*
- *Drawing*
- *Colouring in*
- *Painting*
- *Play dough*
- *Sand play*
- *Water play*
- *Doing a simple jigsaw puzzle*
- *Turn-taking games*
- *Matching games*
- *Lego*
- *Playmobile*
- *Building a tower of bricks*

Undertaking everyday activities can also be helpful in extending a child's concentration span, so you can encourage your child to help around the house. For example:

- *When setting the table, give your child a job to do. Putting the cereal bowls and cutlery on the table, for example.*
- *Helping to clear away after a meal.*

▶ *Putting the shopping in the trolley or basket when at the supermarket.*
▶ *Sorting out the shopping on arriving home.*
▶ *Helping to unload and sort the washing.*
▶ *Packing the bag ready for a day out.*

It does not really matter what it is your child is doing as long as he is enjoying it and you are encouraging him to focus on what he is doing.

3 UNDERSTANDING

Using simple instructions
In addition to the physical skills and the self-help skills your child needs in order to be ready for toilet training, he also needs to have sufficient understanding to be able to follow simple instructions. If he is ready for toilet training, when you say to him 'Do you need a wee?' he will understand that he needs to go and sit on the potty. Give him lots of practice at following instructions, for example:

'Go and get your shoes.'
'Let's find your coat.'
'Where is your toothbrush?'
'Close the door.'
'Can you put that in the bin, please?'

If he is having difficulty following instructions, then show him what you want him to do. Take him by the hand and find his shoes, explaining to him what you are doing. Do this a few times then try asking him again where his shoes are to see if he is developing the understanding.

Using books
Books can also help to develop the understanding that is so vital to successful potty training. Children love simple stories and lots of repetition. There are a number of children's books on the market that will take your child through the routine of using a potty and

help to develop his understanding. Young children love books of this kind because they can identify with them. Using these will reinforce the message that you will be teaching your child during potty training.

All children love to be read to – it is a pleasurable and satisfying activity, which engages the interests and emotions. All books have a message and what better way of using that aspect than reading a book to your child about toilet training.

There are some lovely children's books on the market aimed at exactly this.

Some of the most popular books are mentioned here:

I Want my Potty by Tony Ross (Andersen Press Ltd).

This is probably the most famous book. It charts the story of the little princess and her adventures with the Royal potty.

> *'Nappies are yuuech!' said the little princess.*
>
> *'There must be something better.'*

At first the little princess thinks the Royal potty is even worse than nappies but she soon learns to love it – even if it isn't always there when she needs it.

Parent's comment

My daughter loved this book. I lost track of how often I had to read it to her and we even had to buy a green potty just like in the book for her to use. But it definitely helped with potty training. She soon got the hang of sitting on the potty like the little princess.

Potty Poo-Poo Wee-Wee by Colin McNaughton (Walker Books Ltd).

If your child is fascinated by dinosaurs then this is the book for them. It tells the story of Littlesaurus and his family.

How do you get Littlesaurus to use the potty when he just doesn't want to? And how can you stop him singing 'potty poo-poo wee-wee' in public? The more Mummysaurus and Daddysaurus keep telling him it is rude, the more raucous he gets. Nobody knows what to do, until Daddysaurus gets so frustrated he tells Littlesaurus he doesn't care if he never uses the potty! Which suddenly makes it much more attractive...

Parent's comment

My son just adored this book; it really appealed to his sense of humour. He still laughs at it now and he is almost five.

My Potty Book For Girls/My Potty Book For Boys (Dorling Kindersley).

These last two books, one aimed at boys and the other at girls, are delightful. They tell the story of Mollie and Charlie, who are both nearly two, and how they get to grips with toilet training. One of the nicest things about the Dorling Kindersley books is that they use real photographs. Children really can relate to the pictures because they are realistic. The other lovely thing about these books is that they introduce the idea of pretend play. In the books, each child has a teddy who is also learning how to use the potty. An added extra is that at the end of each book is a page of stickers that you can use on a star chart as an incentive for your child – more about using incentives later in this chapter.

Using pretend play

All children engage in pretend play. It is their way of making sense of the world and will enhance their understanding of many processes that are essential to their life – including that of toilet training.

So, when they dress up in your clothes and put on your shoes, they are not just having fun. They are learning what it is like to be a grown up. Pretending that teddy or dolly is also learning how to use the potty is a great way to get the message across to your child of what is expected of him during the potty training process. It is well worth investing in a toy potty and playing a game where teddy or dolly is learning to sit on the potty and doing a wee or a poo. If you do this once or twice, you will soon find your child holding teddy on the potty – and learning about the toilet training process.

Insight

Using books and pretend play really is a great way to explain to your child just what is expected of them.

Peer group

Children love to copy what they see going on around them – it's how they learn. There is no better way of learning than to watch other people doing what you are expected to learn. In particular, children learn an enormous amount from watching what their peer group and other family members do. So, when you are at home and you are going to the toilet, let your child come with you and see what is happening, explaining as you go along. Let him flush the toilet and watch you wash your hands.

Portia (two years and six months) seemed ready to toilet train, but try as I might she refused point blank to sit on a potty. No amount of bribery worked! I decided to go ahead with the potty training and see what would happen. After breakfast the nappy came off and I would not put one on until four hours later when it was time for her nap. She would hold on to her wee until the nappy went on and then would flood the nappy. Then after nap time the nappy would come off again and then the next time she would wee was when I put her in the bath. We tried to get her to sit on the toilet, but again she refused. This had been going on for a couple of weeks when a little friend of hers came round to play. Millie was four months younger than Portia. During the afternoon, Millie needed to do a wee and went off to use the toilet. Portia followed her and was quite intrigued by all this, especially as she was very aware that she was older than Millie. A little while later Portia announced that she was going to do a wee in the toilet, which she duly did, and there was no looking back.

4 COMMUNICATION

The fourth skill that is essential to successful potty training is that of communication. Your child needs to be able to make himself understood during the process. It is really useful to think about what words you want to use for urine and faeces – we have already touched on this in Chapter 2. You may have pet family names or cultural names for them. By and large most families tend to use the words 'wee' and 'poo' and for the purposes of this book that is what we have decided to use. Start to use the words you have chosen from an early age with your child. So, when you are changing his nappy, tell him that he has done a poo or a big wee. When you are going to the toilet say to him that you are just off to wee.

When he reaches about 18 months of age begin to show him what a poo looks like in his nappy. Can you imagine how frightened a child may feel if the first time he sees a poo is when he does one in the potty? Don't take the chance of your child being worried in this way – get him used to what goes on before he starts to learn to use the potty.

While we're thinking about your child's reaction to poo and so on, you should also take note that it is important to think about your own reaction to soiled nappies – even small babies are sensitive to negative reactions from parents. So, never show disgust at a nappy, even in fun. At the end of this chapter is a case study of a little boy where this happened and it had far-reaching implications for his potty training.

You may also decide that you need to have a discussion about how you are going to name the parts of the body. Some families choose to use the correct anatomical terms but most families will use nicknames or pet names. Again, get your child used to these names well before toilet training begins. Children need to understand what a word means and to have heard it many, many times before they begin to use it themselves. Do this by using lots of repetition and having a little conversation using the words every time you change his nappy or you go to the toilet.

Incentives

In addition to ensuring that your child has all the essential skills in place before you start the potty training process, you as a parent can do your bit. One useful tool in your kit is a system of incentives. All children love incentives and these can come in all shapes and forms and can be used in all sorts of situations.

The easiest incentive has to be praise. Be sure to praise your child whenever he has even a small amount of success in whatever he is doing. Even praise, however, has to be used in the right way. Praising good behaviour and ignoring negative behaviour works best. Children love attention, whether it is positive attention, for example, mum or dad telling them how good they are, or negative attention, for example, mum or dad being cross with them. Either brings them the attention they love. What children don't like is to be ignored. Therefore, if you simply ignore negative behaviour and praise good behaviour they are more likely to behave well.

Rather than just sticking to praising good behaviour, some parents decide to go down the route of rewards when potty training. Think carefully about this, if praise is working well then just stick to that. Try to avoid using items such as sweets, toys and money as incentives, it can often get out of hand and the child can become confused as to why he is getting the extra sweets, toys or money. If you are finding praise on its own is not working, think about using a star chart.

Star charts are a popular incentive for older children. These are probably only useful for children who are older than two and a half years. Children need to be capable of understanding that when they get a certain number of stars or stickers then they will get a treat. If you think this will be a useful incentive to use and that your child will respond to it, it is a good idea to start the star chart before the potty training starts so that he has got the hang of it rather than him having to learn two new things at once. You could use it as an incentive for your child to put his toys away before bed, for example.

To set up a star incentive system, get a large sheet of paper or card and enlist your child's help in decorating it. Next, take your child along to the local toyshop or stationers and let him choose some stickers or stars for the star chart. Again, getting your child involved in making the star chart and choosing the stickers will give him that all-important sense of ownership and control. You should then nominate two or three different activities that you want your child to do. Make them easy and achievable – for example, cleaning his teeth and helping to put on his shoes. Each time he achieves the task, let him choose a sticker and put it on the chart. When he has a certain number of stickers, five for example, he gets a small treat. Keep the treat simple – it does not have to be a trip to Disneyland! Something such as a bowl of ice cream or an extra story at bedtime will do. There is one rule for you to remember – once you have given a sticker, never, ever take it away as this will undo all your good work.

Once he has got the hang of how the star chart works you can then add sitting on the potty to the activities. Once success has been achieved in sitting on the potty, the next task will be doing a wee or a poo in the potty. In this way you will be well on your way to success.

Getting your child used to sitting on the potty

You have bought the potty and you are thinking about starting toilet training, but how do you get your child to sit on the potty?

All children are different, some will just go happily and sit on it, some will give it a go and then lose interest and some will refuse!

Forcing a child to sit on the potty or expecting a child to sit on one for a prolonged amount of time will not work. Sitting on the potty should be done in a relaxed way. Once you have bought your potty, and before toilet training is going to start, leave the potty in the bathroom. When you are next in the bathroom with your child, just casually suggest to your child that he may like to sit on it. Don't make a big fuss if he says no or let him know you feel disappointed. If he wants to sit on the potty with his clothes on or with a nappy on, that is absolutely fine. All you are doing at this stage is getting him used to the potty being around. It needs to become part of everyday life. While he is sitting on the potty you may like to sing a song to him or even read a short story.

The aim very much at this stage is to allow him to feel comfortable about sitting on the potty and to encourage him to stay sitting for a minute or two. Don't forget, if he does sit on the potty, even if it is only for a few seconds, give him lots of praise and tell him how clever he is, with a lovely big hug.

Now, here is the case study mentioned earlier. This focuses on a little boy who had been subjected to negative reactions to a soiled nappy.

Case study: hiding when doing a poo

Junior (three years and two months) lived with his three older brothers and extended family. He was often cared for by his grandparents.

The problem
Junior had been dry since the age of two years and eight months. But he always went and hid when he was doing a poo and would soil his pants.

The reason
After observation and talking to the parents and grandparents it became apparent that all the family members, including his three older siblings, had always made negative comments when Junior had soiled his nappy. So words such as 'stinky' and 'poohy' were used, accompanied by looks of disgust. Of course, at the time this had just been seen as light-hearted fun, but Junior had clearly taken this to heart and it had affected his self-esteem. Another source of embarrassment for Junior was that the potty was left in the living room of the busy household, so he never had privacy when he was having a wee.

The solution
1 *All the family members agreed that they would stop making faces and saying negative things when Junior soiled his pants.*

2 *Junior's parents and grandparents needed to raise his self-esteem.*

3 *Junior needed to be encouraged to sit on the potty when he needed a poo.*

The plan

All the family were involved in following this carefully developed plan:

WEEK ONE

▶ *Whenever Junior did a poo in his pants, it was agreed that no family member would comment. He would be cleaned up and then the incident forgotten.*

▶ *All the family made a special effort to praise Junior whenever possible – for all sorts of things.*

▶ *The potty was moved to the bathroom and Junior was given privacy.*

INTERIM PROGRESS REPORT

It took the family a couple of days to get used to the new rules. But by the end of the week, whenever Junior soiled himself, nobody made a comment. The older siblings really took on the idea of praising Junior and Junior loved all the extra attention from his brothers.

WEEK TWO

▶ *Whenever Junior soiled himself it was quietly suggested to him that he could do his poo in the potty instead of his pants.*

▶ *He was reminded that the potty was in the bathroom and he had privacy when he needed it.*

INTERIM PROGRESS REPORT

Junior's self-esteem was increasing and he seemed much happier that the potty was now in the bathroom and he had privacy. However, he was still soiling his pants.

(Contd)

WEEK THREE

The family continued with Week two rules. The breakthrough came at the end of Week three when there was a large family gathering at the house. Junior needed to do a poo and quietly took himself off to the bathroom and did it on the potty. He then went and found one of his older brothers and told him what he had done. The family waited until the house was quiet and their guests had left. Then they made a big fuss of Junior's success.

The outcome

Junior had developed a negative image of himself when he was doing a poo, and it was compounded every time by the family's reaction, but by developing his self-esteem and stopping the negative comments, the family had changed the situation. With the privacy they had given him and his new sense of control, Junior was able to use his potty successfully.

Conclusion

Young children are often far more aware of what is going on around them than we give them credit for. Children need to be treated with sensitivity and doing something like making fun of a child can have far-reaching consequences.

Frequently asked questions

Q1: *My daughter is 18 months old, I know she is not ready to start toilet training yet, but I am keen to help her on her way. Are there any tips?*

Yes, there are things that you can do to help prepare your child. Getting your daughter used to not wearing a nappy for a short space of time each day is the first. She will have the odd accident, but it will help her to become aware of the sensation of wetness and to make sense of what toilet training is all about. Also, reading books about toilet training to her and engaging in a little pretend play with teddy or dolly sitting on a toy potty will help too.

Q2: *My son is almost three and refuses to sit on the potty. I am pretty sure he understands what he needs to do, but he just will not do it. What can you suggest?*

Try a star chart. He is old enough to understand that if he does something right he can get a reward for it. At first, use the star chart for a couple of easy tasks like teeth cleaning or putting on his shoes. This way he will get lots of attention and stars, then add sitting on the potty with his clothes on. Once he has mastered that, then move on to sitting on the potty with a nappy, then finally without a nappy.

Q3: *My mother-in-law said that when she toilet trained her four boys, she made them sit on the potty until they did something, even if that took half an hour. My son has quite a short attention span and there is no way he will sit for more than a few minutes. How long should a child sit on the potty for?*

Children really only need to sit on the potty for between two and four minutes. That is long enough for them to make the connection between cause and effect. That is the urge to do a wee and then doing it. Most children will get fed up after a few minutes and if you insist on them sitting on the potty for longer you may well put them off altogether.

Summary

This chapter has been all about making sure that you and your child are ready to begin the process of toilet training. You will have considered all the things that you may need to buy before you begin and made your decision about whether to use pants or pull-ups.

Following the 'Toilet readiness questionnaire' in Chapter 2, you will also have reviewed the skills your child needs to start potty training. There is little point in starting the process before your child has all the skills, so spending some time on developing these skills is well worthwhile. When you are confident that your child has mastered the physical, self-help, understanding and communication skills, then you will be ready to start the potty training process. Chapters 4 and 5 will take you through the process of bladder and bowel training step-by-step.

10 THINGS TO REMEMBER

1   *Decide if you are going to use pull-ups or pants. Think about the advantages and disadvantages of each.*

2   *Remember to use appropriate clothing when toilet training: it will make life easier for everyone.*

3   *Decide what equipment you need to buy and have everything ready before you start.*

4   *The first few times you go out while you're toilet training, remember that you need to plan your journey to minimize the risk of accidents.*

5   *Help your child to develop some independence around his physical skills. Begin by teaching him to undress and dress. This will help when he needs to pull down his trousers.*

6   *Help your child to develop his concentration span so that he will be prepared to sit on a potty for a few moments.*

7   *Remember it is really important that children understand what is expected of them. A great way to help them with this is to share books about toilet training and to engage in pretend play.*

8   *Equip your child with the language that they will need to explain what they need to do.*

9   *Remember incentives work very well for some children, especially if they are a little bit older.*

10 *Do some preparation around expecting your child to sit on the potty. Have one around and encourage him to sit on it. It does not matter if he has his clothes on; it is just allowing him to get used to the idea.*

4

The process of toilet training (bladder)

In this chapter you will learn:
- *when it's best to start*
- *about getting started*
- *how to evaluate progress.*

When it's best to start

You and your child have arrived at that exciting point when you've decided to toilet train. You've completed the 'Toilet readiness questionnaire' (see Chapter 2) and found that your child has the skills needed and all the pieces of the jigsaw puzzle are in place. But, before jumping in with both feet, you will need to think about when you are going to start. Choosing a good time to start is essential. A little thought at this point may avoid problems later. Your child may be ready, but are you? Do you recall that in Chapter 2 we outlined when was not an ideal time to start? Let's quickly revisit that list again.

You should avoid starting the potty training process if:

- *your child is going through a negative phase*
- *either the child or the parent is unwell*
- *there is a new baby in the family*
- *your child is starting nursery or play group*

- *you're undergoing a change of childcare*
- *you're going on holiday away from home*
- *you're moving house*
- *there has been a major family upset.*

All of these can upset you or your child – or both – and may well affect the results of your toilet training efforts.

So, we know what would be a bad time to choose to start toilet training, but what would be a good time? Pick a week when family life is quiet. (If your child is ready for toilet training, you will see noticeable progress in a week and by the end of the second week the bulk of the training will be done.) Plan to scale down your usual activities for the first week so that you, as a parent, can concentrate and give your full (or as much as possible) attention to the task in hand. So, if your week usually revolves around lots of outings and activities, plan to give them a miss or scale down to the minimum. A quiet week at home pottering about is ideally what is needed. We all lead very busy lives these days, and that includes our children, but it really is worth investing this time to give your child the opportunity to put all those jigsaw puzzle pieces in place and to make sense of it all. Trying to toilet train when you are dashing off to different activities and when every day there are different demands being made on you and your child is nearly impossible. So, give the outings and groups a miss and allow yourself and your child the time and the space to get on with the task in hand. You will both reap the benefits.

Insight
Choose a quiet week with little activity to do the bulk of your toilet training in.

If you have older children who are at nursery or school, then most of the training will need to be done during the hours that they are out and the house is quiet. So, for example, if you have to do a school or nursery run in the mornings, wait until you get home before you start, then the nappy can come off after you arrive home and then go back on when you go and collect your other children. If, on the other hand, you have a younger child to care for, then that child's needs will have to be fitted around the toilet training. With a younger child around, it is a good idea to plan to restrict the number of rooms used during that week so that you can keep a close eye on both the younger child and the child being trained. Keep a potty in the main room that is used for playing so that it is handy at all times.

Insight
Have two potties (the same colour) – one in the room you will be using most and the other in the bathroom.

It is a good idea to start on a Monday rather than at the weekend, as in most households there tends to be more of a routine during the week than there is at weekends. You will want to keep track of your progress so that you know when you're having success – or when you are not. Keeping a diary is a useful way of assessing progress. It can be helpful in identifying when you need to make changes. We will talk more about this later in this chapter.

Insight
Keep a diary of how toilet training is progressing; it can really help to give you a clear picture of what's happening and whether you need to change any aspect of the training.

Now you've decided exactly when to start the potty training process, let's look at how you can manage what your child eats and drinks during potty training to ensure that this does not have an adverse effect on the process.

Drinks and diet

Parents often worry about how much their child should be drinking during the day. Of course, they want to ensure that their child gets sufficient fluids during the day to be healthy, and adequate fluids are important otherwise your child's urine will become concentrated and this can irritate the bladder.

The recommended daily amount is between six and eight small drinks (150 ml each), which equals about two pints/one litre a day. So, a typical example for the day might be:

On waking	*1 cupful*
Breakfast	*1 cupful plus milk on cereal*
Mid-morning	*1 cupful*
Lunch time	*1 cupful*
Mid-afternoon	*1 cupful*
Tea time	*1 cupful*
Before bed	*1 cupful*

Parents sometimes also worry about exactly what it is best to give their child to drink. Ideal drinks for children are plain tap water and milk. Full-fat milk is suitable as a main drink from one year of age; prior to that it should be breast milk or formula. Full-fat milk is suitable up until five years of age. However, if your child has a varied, balanced diet, you could introduce semi-skimmed milk from the age of two years onwards. Skimmed milk is not suitable for children under the age of five years. Young children need the calories available in full-fat and semi-skimmed milk and also the range of fat-soluble vitamins that are not found in skimmed milk. Fruit juice contains ascorbic acid (vitamin C) and can cause acid erosion of the enamel of young children's teeth, leading to dental decay. If you do give your child fruit juice to drink it should be diluted one part juice to ten parts water and given at meal times. All drinks ideally should be given in a feeder beaker or cup from one year of age instead of from a baby feeding bottle. We are all aware these days that a high sugar intake can cause teeth to decay, so it is advisable not to offer your child sugary drinks and to stick to plain tap water and milk. Drinks that are high in sugar or have caffeine in them can make your child wee more often, which can, of course, make toilet training more problematic.

If you are worried about your child's fluid intake or you feel she needs encouragement to drink more, a bright, fun, drinking bottle with a spout might be the answer. There are lots to choose from, again let your child make the decision about which one to buy; it may be her favourite colour or a character bottle that she likes.

A child can get extra fluids from food as well and below is a list of suggestions.

> **Insight**
>
> If your child is reluctant to drink or if you feel she needs more fluids, try these suggestions:
>
> ▸ *Sugar-free jelly*
> ▸ *Custard*
> ▸ *Rice pudding*
> ▸ *Diluted fruit juice home-made lollies*
> ▸ *Fruit smoothies*
> ▸ *Soup.*

What your child eats is also important when toilet training. In Chapter 5, which deals with the process of toilet training for bowels as opposed to bladder, we will look at the issue of constipation and there is detailed information on how much fibre your child needs plus advice on suitable food sources. If your child is prone to or is, in fact, currently suffering from constipation, it is well worth sorting this out before starting any toilet training, as it can have an impact on training. A child who is constipated may well be reluctant to sit on the potty or may pass urine more frequently because a full bowel can press on the bladder.

> **Insight**
>
> If your child is constipated sort this out before toilet training.

A word about accidents

The vast majority of children will have a number of accidents while they are training and they will still occur even when they are officially 'trained'. Accidents happen for a whole variety of reasons. Children may be just too busy doing something to realize that they need to go to the toilet or they may be in a different place or with different people and don't feel comfortable about asking. Also, it is not uncommon when children are unwell for them to wet themselves.

The best way to deal with ALL accidents is to calmly and quietly clean your child up and don't comment on it, or perhaps say 'maybe next time we can get that in the potty', then just get on with what you were doing. Getting cross or going on about what has happened will not help your child. The vast majority of accidents are just that and they are not the child's fault. If you were learning a new job and made a few mistakes in the first few weeks you would not expect your employer to get cross with you. If your employer did get cross, your self-confidence and self-esteem would soon take a battering and you would begin to worry about doing the job at all.

Insight

Treat all accidents the same. Calmly and quietly clean up your child and just get on with life.

Keeping a diary

As we said previously, it is useful to keep a diary of how toilet training is progressing. Not only will it demonstrate to you if your child is making progress but also it will show you what changes you may need to make to help your child on the way. Below is a suggested format for a daily diary.

DAILY TOILET TRAINING DIARY

Time	Initiated sitting on potty and did a wee or a poo	Prompted to sit on potty and did a wee or a poo	Prompted to sit on potty and did not do a wee	Had an accident	Comments

Write down the time and simply put a tick into whichever box relates to what your child has done. Note any comments that may be useful to you – for example, what was your child doing when the accident happened? Having a picture of what has happened throughout the day will help you plan for the next day and may give you the clues to help your child to succeed quicker.

Twins and triplets

Parents of twins and triplets often ask if they should toilet train their children together to make life easier in terms of mopping up after accidents. But really the children need to be treated as individuals, so although this might sound like more work – two lots of toilet training and two lots of accidents – it will save time in the long run. Because each child is being allowed to progress at her own rate, the toilet training will be less problematic.

Below are a few hints when training twins and triplets:

Top tips for training twins and triplets

▶ *Assess each child's toilet readiness individually, i.e. use one 'Toilet readiness questionnaire' (Chapter 2) for each child.*

▶ *Each child should have her own potty; you may decide to go for the same colour and design or let them each choose their favourite colour.*

▶ *Stick to the same guidelines about potties: one in the bathroom for each child and one in the main play room for each child.*

▶ *Never compare your children in front of each other; this may have a negative effect and prolong toilet training for one of them.*

▶ *If one of the twins or triplets is ready before the other(s), do not make that child wait for their sibling(s) to have acquired the skills.*

In Chapter 7 there is an interesting case study of twins; their
mother attempted to train them at the same time and one of the
girls really rebelled.

Getting started

Once you have made your decision to toilet train, you need to tell
your child what will happen. Let your child know the day before –
bath time is always a good time to chat about things. Children
enjoy bath time and are usually in a relaxed mood. Just tell her
casually that the following day she is going to stop wearing nappies
during the day and will use the potty instead. Don't make a big
fuss about it and don't ask her if she would like to do it. If she
begins to protest be firm about it and then change the subject.

Insight
Bath time is the ideal time to introduce new ideas to your
child as she will be feeling relaxed.

Here's how the first week of potty training might go:

WEEK ONE

Day 1
You will have already decided at what stage of the morning you
will take the nappy off. For example, if the potty training child is
your only child then, after breakfast, take off her nappy and show
her where the potties are. One should be in the bathroom and
another in the room where you will spend most of the morning.
If you have done a nursery or school run then take the nappy off

once you return home. It is very important that you give your child as much of your attention as possible. Watch out for any clues that your child may need to do a wee. For example, you may notice that she is beginning to get a bit fidgety or may be clutching herself (in an effort to stop the wee coming out). Your child should be at the stage of being able to hold on to her urine for one and a half to two hours. If after one to one and a half hours there is no sign that your child needs a wee, gently but firmly say to your child, 'Come on, let's sit on the potty and see if you need a wee'. Then take your child by the hand to the potty and encourage her to sit on the potty for a few minutes. You may decide to read her a short story, sing a song or just simply have a chat. If your child does a wee, give her a lovely warm hug and lots of praise. If she does not do a wee, still praise her for sitting on the potty. If your child has done a wee, then she will probably be OK to go for another one to one and a half hours before needing to sit on the potty again. Don't forget, get into the hang of helping your child to wash and dry her hands whenever she has used the potty (in Chapter 6 there is a section on hand-washing). If she did not do anything then you will need to be very observant for the next hour or so. Try to spot any clues that she may need to go on the potty. Again, for example, look out for her becoming slightly agitated or you may notice her clutching herself. If your child has an accident, then quietly and calmly clean her up and just casually say, 'Next time let's try and do your wee in the potty'.

By now you will be approaching lunchtime and your child will have been without a nappy for three to four hours. During that time she will probably have had two wees and sat on the potty two to three times. There is a real temptation when you are toilet training a child to constantly ask them if they want to do a wee and insist that they sit on the potty frequently. This can be very counterproductive. From your child's point of view there can surely be nothing more irritating than having your parent constantly asking you if you need a wee or insisting that you sit on the potty when you don't need to. Unless your child initiates it in the meantime, then prompting your child to sit on the potty every one to one and a half hours is usually enough. Don't forget, the only person who is in control of this situation is your child. By insisting that she sits on the potty too frequently or by constantly asking her if she needs to, you will give her the impression that you want to be in control and she may decide to rebel.

Keep the diary up – this really will help you have an overall view of what has happened during the day. By the end of a tiring day with children it can be very difficult trying to recollect exactly what happened, at what time, and if there appeared to be a reason for an accident. Having it all written down can be a great reminder as to how the day really went. We often focus on the negative aspects of toilet training and that is, of course, the accidents and also what it feels like if things are not going well. But having it in print where you can see where the successes have happened and where the accidents have happened can help you to help your child.

Most children at the age that toilet training is happening will still be having an after-lunch nap. So, once lunch is over, offer the potty again and then pop on a nappy for her lunchtime sleep. Explain to her that when she is asleep she needs to have the nappy on, so that she does not feel that you are giving her mixed messages.

Don't be surprised if your child wees in the nappy straight away; don't forget for the last two to three years that is what she has always done. After she has woken up from her sleep, take off the nappy and take her to sit on the potty. If the nappy is dry, praise her, but don't worry if it is not. The afternoon will progress much the same as the morning. Take your child to the potty every one to one and a half hours right up to when you give her a bath and put on the last nappy of the day, and don't forget the diary. The following is an example of how your day might look:

A TYPICAL FIRST DAY TOILET TRAINING:

7 a.m.	Wakes. Drink of milk. Fresh nappy.
8 a.m.	Breakfast with drink.
8.30 a.m.	Take off nappy. Sit on potty.
9.30–10 a.m.	Sit on potty.
11 a.m.	Mid-morning drink/snack and sit on potty.
12.30 p.m.	Sit on potty. Lunch/drink.
	(Contd)

1–2/3 p.m.	Nappy on/sleep.
2.30/3 p.m.	Mid-afternoon drink/snack and sit on the potty.
4–4.30 p.m.	Sit on potty.
5.30 p.m.	Tea and drink. Sit on potty.
6.30 p.m.	Bath and fresh nappy on. Drink before bed.

At bath time, chat to your child about all the positive things that have happened today and what she has enjoyed. During the conversation talk about how it was using the potty – but only talk about any positive aspects of the training. So, for example, if she was really good about sitting on the potty, chat about that and tell her how proud you were of her. If there were any successes in the potty, again use lots of praise. Get the family involved, if older siblings have been at nursery or school, tell them about your child's successes and tell your partner as soon as they arrive home if they have been out working. A phone call to grandparents to let your child tell them about their day is also a lovely way to reinforce to your child how well she is doing and how proud everyone feels about her.

Hopefully you will be keeping a diary at this stage, as it is useful for monitoring how often your child wees, what the pattern is and how many accidents or successes your child has. At the end of Day 1, when your child has gone to bed, look at the diary and review how the day has gone. What have been the successes? Think how you can build on those.

Ask yourself these questions:

▶ *Are there signs that my child is understanding what is expected of her?*
▶ *Is she happy to sit on the potty?*
▶ *Is there a reasonable amount of time between wees?*
▶ *Have there been any successes during the day?*
▶ *Do I have to prompt her every time?*
▶ *Have I been able to pick up on any clues that my child displays which tell me she needs to use the potty?*
▶ *Is there anything that I need to do differently on Day 2?*

Days 2 and 3

Day 2 and Day 3 will progress pretty much as Day 1. At this point you need to build on your successes, so if your child has done well sitting on the potty, remember to reinforce that and give her lots and lots of praise. Try again to keep the days quiet and stress free, with lots of pottering about the home. Remember that you will need to take her to the potty every one to one and a half hours unless she is beginning to initiate it herself, and also to keep the diary going so that you can see the progress. At bath time you can again reinforce all the good stuff that happened during the day, including any successes with the toilet training.

Evaluating progress

At the end of Day 3, once your child has gone to bed, you need to evaluate the progress that she has made. This is the half-way mark for the first week, so if your child is ready to be trained you will certainly have seen some progress in the last three days. You will probably see in your Daily Toilet Training Diary that there are more ticks in the first and second boxes and fewer in the accident box. If you find that there have been plenty of successes, then your child understands (or is beginning to understand) what is expected of her and you are both well on the way. You need to keep building on all that your child has achieved in the last three days. It is still early days and accidents can continue to happen for some time but remember what was said earlier on – treat all accidents the same and don't get cross, just clean your child up and get on with life.

What if training is not going well?

If, after three days, you find that your child is constantly having accidents and that the pieces of the jigsaw puzzle don't seem to have fallen into place you need to re-evaluate what has been happening.

Ask yourself these questions:

▶ *Have the past three days been quiet and stress free to allow me and my child to focus on the task in hand?*

> ► *Have I kept the diary to be able to build up a picture of how the toilet training process has been going?*
> ► *What successes have we had?*

In the great scheme of things, three days is a short time span. If your child was showing all the signs of toilet readiness before you started, there will have been some positives in the last three days. Do make sure life is quiet and that you and your child are able to potter around, which will allow you to give your child the attention that she needs. Build on any success that your child has had and if you have not been keeping a dairy, think about doing so. For some children it just takes a little longer for the penny to drop and for all the pieces of the jigsaw puzzle to fit into place.

Days 4 and 5
Your child has made progress in the last three days, and you need to continue building on that by gently starting to give her more of a sense of independence by letting her decide when she needs to go to the toilet (if she has not started to initiate this herself already). Some children will initiate going to the toilet themselves quite early on in the toilet training process, whereas others will need a helping hand. It does not matter if they do need help in this department. So, instead of taking your child to the potty every one to one and a half hours, wait and see if she starts to ask herself. Begin talking to her about if she has that feeling that she needs to do a wee. You can start to give her the confidence to begin to make the decision for herself to go and use the potty. Remember to give lots and lots of praise at all successes – no matter how small – and don't forget to share those successes with the family.

Days 6 and 7
By now your child really will have made noticeable progress. She will be having more successes than accidents and will probably be initiating going to the toilet without any prompting from you. However, don't worry if she is still having the odd accident; it is totally normal at this stage. You can think about the next step during these final two days of the first week, i.e. your child going out without a nappy. There are two schools of thought about going

out without a nappy and you need to decide which one suits you and your child.

One school of thought is that once you start the toilet training process, putting a nappy back on the child at any time (except nap times and night time) is giving your child mixed messages. If you decide to go down this route then you do need to be prepared for accidents outside the home in the early days. Toilet training at home, where it is quiet and stress free and where there is a potty on hand, is very different to being outside where there are lots of distractions. You may be in a shop or a car when your child decides she needs a wee and – guess what – there will be no potty on hand.

The other school of thought is that children adapt well to different situations and will not get mixed messages from having a nappy on for a short amount of time in the early days for a trip out to the shops or for the nursery or school run. Don't forget this is a major leap in your child's development and it may be a little too much to expect it all to fit into place straight away. If you decide that, in the early days, your child will wear a nappy for any short trips outside the home, a suggested way forward is given below. Until you feel confident for any trips outside the home, pop a nappy back on. If, towards the end of the first week, training has gone well, then you can think about a short trip out without a nappy.

Going out without a nappy
If you have started training on a Monday, then Days 6 and 7 will fall at the weekend and now is the time to let your child go out without a nappy on a short trip. Don't forget to explain in advance to your child that this is going to happen. Plan your trip carefully, for example, a short trip to the local shops or perhaps to a friend's house will be far easier than a long car journey. Before going out make sure that your child has had ample opportunity to do a wee. By now you will have a rough idea as to how long your child can go between wees, so you can make sure that you are back home within that time span (or alternatively, you will have arrived at your friend's house). If you have decided to purchase a fold-away potty

with a disposable liner for trips out, do make sure that your child has had the opportunity to sit on it at home before you expect her to use it outside the home and don't forget to take spare clothing just in case of an accident. Above all, remember the golden rule – never, ever, get cross if your child has an accident. Just clean her up and get on with life. Once you have done a couple of short trips and you are feeling confident, you can begin to do slightly longer ones.

Insight

If you are going to use a fold-away potty for trips out, let your child try it out before she is expected to use it. She will feel far more comfortable using it outside the home if she is familiar with it before you go out with it for the first time.

Don't forget to take a change of clothing when planning those early trips out without a nappy.

WEEK TWO

How the second week progresses will really hinge on the degree of success that your child reached during the first week of training. If the first week has gone really well (and for some children a week will show really good progress) then your second week will be about fine-tuning.

Again, scale down the week in terms of activities but you can start to re-introduce a regular routine. So if, for example, your child attends a parent and toddler group or maybe a music group, go along but make sure that you are well prepared. Before leaving the house make sure your child has ample opportunity to do a wee, take spare clothes with you and, as soon as you arrive, check out the toilets. Most venues that hold children's groups or activities will have a potty in the toilets, but if you have a fold-away potty be sure to take it with you. If you are out and about in the early days of toilet training you will certainly need to be more aware of your child's toileting needs. Your child will be exposed to lots of distractions and may be just too busy to realize that she needs a wee, or she may become anxious that if she goes for a wee someone will take the toy that she was playing with. So, be observant for those signs that she may need a wee – you know, when they jiggle about or start to clutch themselves. If you see these signs, firmly but gently take your child by the hand and tell her that she needs a wee.

If you feel that your child is not quite ready for lots of activity, that's fine – just continue with a second quiet week and aim to build on all the successes of the previous week. For some children it just takes that bit longer for it all to fall into place.

By the end of the second week, real progress will be seen. Some children will be clean and dry with just the odd accident, while for others there may still be accidents on a regular basis but they are getting the idea and there are some successes.

If you feel that neither of the above scenarios describe your child and she is still having lots of accidents and only very few successes, then this may well not be the right time to train your child. Pop your child back into nappies. This is not a failure; it is purely and simply that your child was not ready. Continuing to train when a child is clearly not ready can be very counterproductive. Both you and your child will become very stressed and it may prolong the toileting process unnecessarily. It is much better to pop your child back into nappies for a month or so and then, as long as you are sure that they have toilet readiness, have another go.

Boys standing up to wee

When boys first start to train they will do a wee sitting down because that is the easiest way to do it. But there will come a time when it will be helpful for them to learn to wee standing up. For some boys this will not be an issue and they will adapt quickly, but others may need a little help with developing their aim. A role model is really helpful in guiding them on how to wee standing up. So a dad or older male sibling or friend can be a great example. Below are a few fun ideas for helping their aim.

Case study: refusing to sit on the potty

Toyne (two years and eight months) was the third child in the family. She had two older brothers and was looked after full-time by her mother.

The problem

Toyne's mother had already attempted to toilet train her daughter when she was two years and three months old. It had been a total disaster and since then Toyne had refused to sit on the potty. Toyne's mother really did not know what to do next. She felt that her daughter had a very stubborn streak and that toilet training had become a battleground.

The reason

There was a real battle of wills going on between Toyne and her mother. Toyne wanted to train in her own good time but her mother was very keen to get on with it and for it to be done and dusted as quickly as possible. Toyne rebelled strongly against this and the situation had become very tense between mother and daughter.

The solution

We needed to find out if Toyne was now ready for toilet training so that, if she had toilet readiness, we could put a plan in place. Toyne's parents completed the toilet readiness questionnaire and yes, their daughter did have all the skills in place. It was decided that incentives – in the form of a star chart – would form a major part of the plan and that things would be taken slowly.

The plan
WEEK ONE
A star chart was started with three activities on it:

1 *Clean teeth.*
2 *Wash hands before meals.*
3 *Sit on the potty fully clothed and with a nappy on.*

Toyne was asked to just sit on the potty before breakfast, lunch and tea. She was allowed to sit on the potty with a nappy on and fully clothed. She was not expected to do anything in her nappy. Every time she sat on the potty she was rewarded with a short story book while sitting on the potty and a star for her star chart afterwards. This was continued for a week.

WEEK TWO
During Week two the star chart and story-telling continued with Toyne being asked to sit on the potty with just a nappy on.

INTERIM PROGRESS REPORT
By the end of the second week, Toyne was happy to sit on the potty with just a nappy on. However, her mother was becoming quite frustrated by what she saw as a lack of progress, but when it was pointed out to her that two weeks ago she could not even get Toyne to sit on a potty, on reflection she did realize that Toyne had made great advances.

WEEK THREE
It was agreed that using a toilet training diary and star chart that included toilet training could be commenced. Toyne's mother agreed somewhat reluctantly to scale down their activities for that week and to concentrate on toilet training.

INTERIM PROGRESS REPORT
Days 1, 2 and 3 of Week three did not reap much success. Toyne did agree to sit on the potty at regular intervals but continued to have accidents. By the end of Day 3, Toyne's mother was ready to

(Contd)

throw in the towel and needed an enormous amount of persuasion to continue. But at the end of Day 4, Toyne did her first ever wee on the potty. Success!

By the end of the following week (Week four) Toyne was clean and dry during the day.

The outcome

It took four weeks to toilet train Toyne. Her mother found the process very frustrating and realized, on reflection, that it was Toyne in charge and not her.

Conclusion

Toyne clearly felt the pressure from her mother to train. If there had been less pressure and a more relaxed approach from Toyne's mother, she would probably have trained much more quickly. This shows just how important parents' attitudes can be in the toilet training process. A child needs to feel that she is in control and will often – as in Toyne's case – react badly to any perceived pressure.

Frequently asked questions

Q1: *I am expecting another baby in two months time and I am thinking about toilet training my daughter before the baby arrives so that I do not have to deal with two lots of nappies. Is this a good idea?*

Toilet training a toddler just before a new baby is due may present you with some difficulties. The vast majority of young children will react when a new baby arrives and it is not uncommon for newly toilet-trained children to regress and start wetting. Also, you are likely to be very busy in the first few months after the new baby arrives and dealing with accidents may become very stressful. Why not wait until the baby is about four months old and more settled? That way you will be able to give the toilet training the attention it will need.

Q2: *My daughter is driving me mad. She has been toilet trained for a few months now, but I have to remind her all the time to do* *a wee or she ends up having an accident. How can I get her to take the initiative?*

Make sure that your daughter is drinking enough – at least six to eight small drinks evenly spaced throughout the day. If her urine is concentrated, it may be irritating her bladder. Get her into a routine of going to the toilet every two hours, so she begins to understand the feeling of a full bladder. Once you have established the routine, talk to her about what it feels like to need a wee, so that she learns to pick up the clues that she needs to go to the toilet.

Q3: *My son is beginning to get the idea about sitting on the potty but we still have not had any wees in it. What tends to happen is that he sits on the potty then gets up and a few minutes later has an accident. Any ideas?*

Continue to encourage him to sit on the potty as you have been doing, but every time he has an accident sit him back on the potty while you clean up. Very gently say to him, the potty is where you need to do the wee. It may be that he has not quite made the connection. By getting him to sit on the potty after having an accident it will reinforce the idea that the potty is where you do a wee.

Summary

This chapter has been about the nuts and bolts of toilet training. The important message to take away with you is that you must be prepared to give your full attention to the task in hand.

If a child is ready to toilet train, with all the skills in place, and you have found a calm time with no changes about to happen in her life, then there should be success within a week or two. If this success is not happening then it is best to pop your child back into nappies, leave it a month and then try again. The next chapter covers bowel training, which will usually happen at the same time as the bladder training.

10 THINGS TO REMEMBER

1 *Think about when is the best time to start. The following times are best avoided:*
    Your child is going through a negative phase.
    Either the child or the parent is unwell.
    There is a new baby in the family.
    Your child is starting nursery or playgroup.
    You're undergoing a change of childcare.
    You're going on holiday away from home.
    You're moving house.
    There has been a major family upset.

2 *Remember to have a quiet week with little activity to do the bulk of your toilet training in. If you are working outside the home, think about having a week off.*

3 *Have two potties in the same colour. Keep one in the room you will be using most and the other in the bathroom.*

4 *Make sure your child is drinking plenty as concentrated urine can make the bladder very irritable. Ideal drinks are milk and water.*

5 *Remember – be prepared for accidents. It is a normal part of the toilet training process.*

6 *Keeping a diary can be very helpful in planning the process and is a good way to reflect on progress.*

7 *Once you have decided to start toilet training it is important to talk to your child about what is going to happen.*

8 *Remember to evaluate progress at the end of each day and reflect on how it has gone. This will help you to see if you need to make any changes.*

9 Remember, if training is not going well it may be that your child is simply not ready. There is nothing wrong with putting a child back into nappies and leaving the training for a month before trying again.

10 Boys need to learn to wee standing up. Having a role model that they can observe is a great help.

5

The process of toilet training (bowels)

In this chapter you will learn:
- *about constipation and diet*
- *when it's best to start*
- *how to get started.*

Children are often clean before they are dry for the simple reason that young children tend to poo only once or twice a day and obviously have a bit more notice when they need to do a poo than when they need to wee. Therefore it is often easier to catch a poo (stool) than a wee. Also they tend to be quite regular when they need to do a poo, maybe after breakfast or lunch.

Before starting to toilet train your child, it is very important to ensure he is not constipated. Constipation can be common in children aged between two and four years, the peak time for toilet training. If you think your child is suffering from constipation it is well worth discussing the problem with your health visitor or GP to sort out the issue before training begins. Trying to train a child who is suffering from constipation may well make the matter much worse. In this chapter there is a detailed section on what constipation is, what signs to look for and how to resolve the problem by increasing the amount of fibre in your child's diet. So, if you are in any doubt whether your child is constipated, have a chat with your health visitor or GP for advice.

Diet and constipation

Many children get constipated from time to time for a variety of reasons but not usually because there is anything physically wrong with them.

Insight
Up to ten per cent of children are thought to suffer constipation at any one time.

The facts about constipation and children are startling. About one third of four- to seven-year-olds are constipated at any one time and in fact, five per cent of primary school children get constipated for more than six months. Chronic constipation is most common in children between the ages of two and four – just when they are potty training.

With constipation being so widespread, it is obviously a subject that will affect many parents during the toilet training period in their children's lives and, if we can appreciate exactly what the problem is and its effects, we can deal with it more effectively and, perhaps, head off any possible problems in this area.

So, what is constipation? Constipation is when your child does not have a bowel movement often enough – that is having a poo fewer than three times a week. This can be the start of the problem because then, of course, when they have a poo it can hurt as the stools have become hard and dry. It is important to note at this point, however, that there are also some children who appear to be doing a poo every day, but, in fact, they are not emptying their bowel properly and are only passing very small amounts of stool. So these children can also be classed as suffering from constipation.

How to tell if your child may be constipated

Some signs to look out for are:

- *Fewer bowel movements than expected (three times per week or less often).*
- *Pain and straining on passing stools.*
- *Tummy ache.*
- *Small, dry, hard stools.*
- *Avoiding the toilet.*
- *Not having an urge to do a poo.*
- *Feeling that a bowel movement isn't finished.*
- *Sore bottom.*
- *Unpleasant smell.*
- *Dribbling urine.*
- *Leaking of liquid or loose stool.*

How constipation develops

The causes of constipation will differ from child to child and in some cases there may be a combination of factors contributing to the problem. Constipation can happen suddenly (for example, after a child has been unwell and not eaten or drunk properly for a few days) or it can happen slowly without anyone being aware that it is happening.

Let's look at a typical case of how constipation can develop. For some children, just one painful experience of pushing out a hard, dry stool can cause them to become afraid of doing a poo again. This can get your child into the habit of avoiding going to the toilet in case it hurts. Children can become quite determined in this situation and they may start to hold in stools by tightening the muscles around the anus to keep it closed and put off the urge to poo. Of course, this only makes the problem worse because the stool starts to build up in the child's bowel then the build up of stools in the rectum causes it to stretch, making it harder for the child to feel the urge to poo. At this point, the child may need to strain when he goes to the toilet and will find it hard to relax enough to do a poo – making the constipation worse. In later stages of constipation, large stools may get stuck and block the child's bowel. Liquid stools above this blockage then flow around it and the child may leak watery stools.

Risk factors for constipation

As we have said, there are lots of reasons why constipation may develop and it may be helpful to check this list if you see any signs of constipation in your child:

▶ **Dietary factors** – *not drinking enough water or eating enough high-fibre food can cause stools to become dry and hard to pass.*
▶ **Holding on to stools** – *sometimes a child can hold on too long, perhaps because they don't want to stop what they are doing, for example, a game.*
▶ **Changes in daily routine** – *changes such as going on holiday, moving house, changing childcare or a new baby in the house can all affect your child's routine and, in turn, upset his natural bowel rhythm and cause constipation.*
▶ **Not enough exercise** – *lack of physical activity can cause your child's bowel to become more sluggish and lead to constipation.*
▶ **Constipation in your family** – *if other family members suffer from constipation, this can increase your child's risk of becoming constipated.*
▶ **Medicines** – *some medicine can cause constipation.*

Preventing and treating constipation

With so many reasons and factors affecting constipation, there are obviously lots of things that you can do to prevent and treat the condition in your child:

▶ *One of the most important factors in treating and preventing constipation is diet and the amount of fibre in it. There will be plenty more information on this in the next section of this chapter.*

▶ *Don't let your child wait to do a poo. If you pick up a clue that your child needs to do a poo, make sure that he sits on the potty or toilet as soon as possible. Simply ask him, in a matter of fact way, 'Do you need to do a poo?' – don't let his preoccupation with a game or other goings-on cause a delay.*

▶ *Give your child enough time so they don't feel rushed. Set aside a time each day for your child to sit on the potty or toilet – perhaps after breakfast or lunch. You will, by this time, have had plenty of opportunity to observe his bowel habits, so pick the best time to suit him and make sure he isn't made to feel in a hurry.*

▶ *Make going to the toilet fun by keeping special treats reserved for the toilet such as a favourite book or getting him to blow bubbles.*

▶ *It is important that your child sits properly on the potty or toilet. He should have his knees bent and his feet either flat on the floor or resting on a step. Any other position can lead to constipation, as your child's bowels may not be allowed to empty properly.*

▶ *If your child says that it hurts to poo, tell him to stop trying and then try again later.*

▶ *Encourage your child to get lots of active play to increase bowel activity.*

Insight

If your child suffers from constipation, you really do need to sort this out before you start training. Once you have sorted out the constipation, keep up the fibre content of your child's diet and make sure he is drinking plenty every day to prevent it happening again.

Increasing dietary fibre

Diet is particularly important in preventing and treating constipation – eating foods that are high in fibre increases the bulk of the stools. This makes them softer by helping them retain water and so they are easier to push out. Making it easier and more comfortable for your child to pass a poo is vital, so here are a few ways to increase dietary fibre:

▶ *Try to include a variety of high-fibre foods in the family's daily diet, such as wholegrain cereals, wholegrain pasta and rice, wholemeal or granary breads, and plenty of fruit and vegetables.*
▶ *Fruit and vegetables should include dried fruit and fruit eaten with the skin on as well as vegetables, particularly beans, peas, sweetcorn and pulses such as lentils.*

How much fibre does your child need?

Here's how to calculate how much fibre (in grams) your child should be eating per day:

Take your child's age in years and add five grams for children older than two years.

For example, if your child is three years old, then the calculation would be 3 + 5 = 8, therefore a three-year-old child should be eating eight grams of fibre a day. (See table below for what this could be made up of.)

Insight
Read the food packaging on food items to work out if it's a food rich in fibre.

Increasing fluid intake

In addition to ensuring that your child has sufficient fibre in his diet, it is important to make sure that his fluid intake is adequate.

This is because raising a child's fluid intake increases the water content of the stools and this, in turn, makes them softer and easier to pass. Again, the aim is to keep things as comfortable and as easy as possible for your child.

▶ *Encourage your child to drink six to eight glasses of fluid each day. This is approximately two pints/one litre per day.*
▶ *For school-aged children, ask their teacher about bringing a bottle of water into school each day.*

Here is a list of fibre-rich foods in various categories that will help you to make choices about which foods to include in your child's diet to ensure that constipation does not become a problem (or to include if you're trying to treat constipation).

Food	Portion size	Fibre content (grams)
Bread		
Brown	1 small slice	0.9
High-fibre white	1 small slice	0.8
Hovis	1 small slice	0.8
Wholemeal	1 small slice	1.5
Wholemeal pitta bread	1 small slice	1.8
Breakfast cereals		
All-Bran	Average small bowl	7.2
Bran Buds	Average small bowl	6.6
Bran Flakes	Average small bowl	2.6
Country Store	Average small bowl	1.2
Fruit 'n' Fibre	Average small bowl	1.4
Mini Shredded Wheat	Average small bowl	3.4
Muesli	Average small bowl	2.0
Porridge	Average small bowl	2.5
Raisin Splitz	Average small bowl	2.3
Sultana Bran	Average small bowl	2.0
Weetabix	1 biscuit	1.9

Food	Portion size	Fibre content (grams)
Biscuits and pastry		
Cereal bar	1	1.0
Cracker (wholemeal)	1	0.4
Digestive (plain)	1	0.3
Gingernuts	1	0.2
Oat-based biscuit	1	0.5
Oatcakes	1	0.7
Shortbread	1	0.2
Wholemeal scone	1 average size	2.6
Wholemeal fruit cake	Average slice	1.7
Fruit (raw)		
Avocado pear	Half pear	2.6
Banana	1 medium	1.1
Blackberries	10	1.5
Dates (dried)	5	3.0
Eating apples	1 small	1.3
Fruit cocktail (canned in juice)	Small bowl	1.2
Grapefruit	Half grapefruit	1.0
Grapes	10	0.6
Kiwi fruit	1 medium	1.1
Mango	1 slice	1.0
Melon (cantaloupe)	1 slice	1.5
Orange	1 small	2.0
Peach	1 small	1.1
Pear	1 medium	3.3
Pineapple	1 large slice	1.0
Plum	1 small	0.5
Prunes (dried)	5	2.3
Raisins	1 tablespoon	0.6
Raspberries	10	1.0
Strawberries	5	0.7
Sultanas	1 tablespoon	0.5
Tangerine	1 small	0.6
		(Contd)

Food	Portion size	Fibre content (grams)
Nuts (whole nuts should not be given to children under five years due to the risk of choking)		
Almonds	6 whole	1.0
Brazils	6 whole	0.6
Peanuts	10 whole	0.8
Peanut butter	Thickly spread on 1 slice of bread	1.4
Rice and pasta		
Brown boiled rice	2 heaped tablespoons	0.6
Wholemeal spaghetti	3 tablespoons	3.1
Vegetables		
Baked beans	2 tablespoons	3.0
Beetroot	4 slices	0.8
Broad beans	2 tablespoons	7.8
Broccoli tops (raw)	2 spears	2.4
Butter beans	2 tablespoons	3.7
Cabbage	2 tablespoons	1.1
Carrots	2 tablespoons	2.0
Cauliflower	3 florets	0.5
Celery (raw)	1 stick	0.3
Chickpeas	2 tablespoons	2.9
Corn-on-the-cob	1 whole	2.7
Green pepper	2 slices rings	0.3
Leeks	Stem, white portion only	1.1
Lentils split (boiled)	2 tablespoons	1.5
Peas	2 tablespoons	3.0
Potatoes (baked)	1 small with skin	2.7
Potatoes (new)	2 average size	1.2
Red kidney beans	2 tablespoons	4.3
Spinach	2 tablespoons	1.7
Sweetcorn (canned)	2 tablespoons	0.9
Tomatoes (raw)	1 small	0.7
Turnip	1 tablespoon	0.8

Typical daily diet for a three-year-old

This is a suggested menu for a typical three-year-old. If you have a child who is prone to constipation, he may need a little more fibre in his diet than the average child of his age.

This day's menu would be suitable for an average three-year-old who does not suffer from constipation. When planning your child's diet it is useful to look at the fibre content of the foods that you are giving him. Get into the habit of checking the fibre content on the back of food packaging. Most people assume that all breakfast cereal is full of fibre but, for example, cornflakes have only 0.2 grams of fibre for an average bowl whereas Mini Shredded Wheat has 3.4 grams and Weetabix 1.9 grams per biscuit. So, it is important to make choices that will add up to the daily-required amount of fibre.

The following menu for the day adds up to 9.3 grams – an average three-year-old needs 8 grams. It gives a little leeway in case all portions are not finished.

Meal	Grams of fibre
Breakfast	
One biscuit of Weetabix with full-fat milk	1.9
An apple	1.3
Mid-morning snack	
A portion of grapes (10)	0.6
Lunch	
Ham sandwich made with two slices of wholemeal bread with cucumber on the side and a full-fat yoghurt	3.5
Mid-afternoon snack	
One small snack-size box of raisins and two rice cakes	0.6

(Contd)

Dinner

Pasta with tomato sauce and grated cheese	0.7
Ice cream and fresh strawberries	0.7

Total amount of fibre is 9.3 grams

If you find your child is reluctant to eat a variety of high-fibre foods, here are a few suggestions.

▶ *Dried fruit is a great source of fibre; if you find your child is reluctant there is now a whole range of yoghurt-covered dried fruit available from supermarkets and health food shops, which often appeal to children.*

▶ *A great way to increase the fibre content of Weetabix or porridge, and which works wonders with constipation, is to make an apricot purée. Soak dried apricots overnight; in the morning cook them in water until soft and then whiz up in a liquidiser until very smooth. This purée can be stored in the fridge for a few days and a spoonful added to breakfast cereal or served with yoghurt.*

▶ *Finally, if your child likes tomato sauce, soak red lentils overnight, and then cook in water until mushy. Add the cooked lentils to the tomato sauce and again put through the liquidiser until smooth. Serve as a topping for pasta or as a base for home-made pizza.*

When to see your GP

If your child is suffering from constipation and an increase in fibre and fluids in his diet are not helping, then you really do need to seek the advice of your GP. It may be that your child will need stool softening medication to help deal with the problem and your GP will be able to advise you. Your child should also always see his GP if for any reason there is blood in his poo. Sometimes a hard poo can cause a tear in the skin around the anus and blood can be seen on the poo or in the potty or toilet. This can be very painful and distressing for the child and your GP may want to prescribe a stool softener to stop this from happening again and to allow the tear to heal. In severe cases of constipation, a child can begin to soil, as we see in the next section.

Childhood soiling

Soiling usually happens when a child has become constipated and a large, hard poo is blocking the rectum. A bit of the poo may break off and soil the child's pants or liquid poo from behind the large, hard poo can leak around and stain the pants.

Soiling is not done on purpose and usually the child will not know it has happened until afterwards.

It is thought that regular soiling occurs in about:

1 in 30 children between the ages of 4 and 5 years
1 in 50 children between the ages of 5 and 6 years
1 in 75 children between the ages of 6 and 10 years
1 in 100 children between the ages of 10 and 12 years
(Source: Doleys et al. 1981)

So, as you can see, it is not that uncommon a problem. It does tend to happen to more boys than girls but no one knows why that is.

It can understandably cause enormous upset and stress for the child and family.

If your child is suffering from soiling, it is wise to arrange an appointment with your family doctor. Many cases of soiling are due to constipation, which your family doctor will be able to treat.

We will talk about soiling in more detail in Chapters 7 and 9, with steps that you can take to help deal with the issue.

The process of toilet training – getting started

Insight

Keep a diary of your child's bowel habits so that you can anticipate when they are likely to do a poo – then aim to sit them on the potty around this time each day.

The same advice in terms of when to start applies to bowel training as to bladder training. Obviously the training runs side by side but, as we said earlier, children are often clean before they are dry. The most important issue is that if there are any signs of constipation, it is dealt with before training starts. Once constipation has been tackled it is important to keep up the fibre and fluid content of the diet so your child does not become constipated again.

Insight

Children often gain bowel control before they gain bladder control. You can help this by encouraging a good bowel routine, i.e. the same time each day. This will make bowel training so much easier.

Some children do not like the sensation of poo coming away from them. Nappies offer a nice firm base to push against when you are doing a poo, so it can feel very strange not having that there. So you may need to do an extra bit of reassurance when the poo comes out or, if your child really is not very keen, let him keep the nappy on to do the poo but encourage him to sit on the potty (complete with nappy) when doing it in the first instance until his confidence grows.

Insight

Let your child see his poo before you start any training so he does not get a fright the first time he does one in a potty and sees it.

WEEK ONE

Day 1

Look for any sign that may tell you your child is getting ready to do a poo, for example:

▶ *standing very still*
▶ *grunting*
▶ *squatting*
▶ *going red in the face.*

If you see any of these signs, act quickly and pop him on the potty. If he is regular, be especially aware around the usual times that he does a poo. It is a good idea, if he is sitting on the potty at that time, to encourage him to sit for an extra couple of minutes. Do not rush him as this can put children off big time! If you have a success let him see what he has done – poo in a potty does look different to poo in a nappy. Take the potty to the toilet and show him how you flush the poo away, this will help him to make sense of the process when he eventually uses the toilet. Then, as you do after he has done a wee on the potty, help him to wash and dry his hands.

Make a note of the time he did the poo and add any successes in the comments section of your toilet training diary. Remember the golden rule – if any accident happens, don't get cross, just clean him up and gently say that next time maybe he can do that in the potty.

And don't forget lots of praise for any successes.

Days 2 and 3

Days 2 and 3 will pretty much follow as Day 1. Build on any successes that you may have and keep the diary up to date – it can be a great tool to assess progress and as an aid to deciding if your approach is working.

Evaluating progress

Again, as with bladder training, at the end of Day 3 think about how the training has been progressing. Often children are clean before they are dry simply because a child does not poo as often as they wee and they generally have more notice and time to get to the potty. If your child is ready to train, you may well have had a few successes with poos in the potty but don't worry if there have been a couple of accidents – it is still early days.

If your child is having accidents in this area, ask yourself these questions:

▶ *Is my child constipated?*
▶ *Am I giving him enough time to sit on the potty?*
▶ *Does he feel uncomfortable about letting go?*

If you feel that maybe your child is not making the connection between the potty and doing a poo, what you can try doing is when he has an accident, pop him on the potty while you are clearing up and gently say to him 'poo goes in the potty'. This can help to reinforce that poos go in the potty and to make that connection. If you feel that your child feels uncomfortable about letting go, then do let him have a nappy on to do the poo but encourage him to sit on the potty while doing the poo. You can then slowly work towards removing the nappy.

Days 4 and 5

Your child has made progress in the last three days, and you need to continue building on that. You need to gently start giving your child more of a sense of independence by letting him decide when he needs to go to the toilet. So wait and see if he starts to initiate it himself. Begin talking to him about whether he has that feeling that he needs to do a poo. You can start to give him the confidence to begin to make the decision himself to go and use the potty. Remember to give lots and lots of praise at all successes – no matter how small.

Days 6 and 7

By now your child really will have made noticeable progress. He will be having more successes than accidents and will probably be initiating going to the toilet without any prompting from you. However, don't worry if he is still having the odd accident – it is totally normal at this stage. You can think about the next step during these final two days of the first week, i.e. your child going out without a nappy.

Going out without a nappy
In the early days of going out without a nappy, it is likely to be less stressful for your child if the planned trip does not coincide with the time that he is likely to do a poo if that can be anticipated. However, it is a good idea to take some baby wipes just in case a poo does happen. Again, if you are planning on using a fold-away potty or child toilet seat when you are out, ideally let your child use it at home first so he has got used to it.

WEEK TWO

Again, as with bladder training, how Week two will progress will depend very much on the successes of Week one. If the first week has gone well, then you can begin to re-introduce more activity in Week two. Be aware of the times when your child is most likely to do a poo and ensure where possible that he feels comfortable about doing his poo if he is out and about. Remember – never rush a child when they are doing a poo as it can cause the bowel not to completely empty, which may in turn lead to constipation.

Insight
When your child is doing a poo, encourage him to sit slightly forward. This helps to open up the pelvic area and empty the bowel completely.

Case study: will only do a poo in a nappy

Ella (two years and four months) was an only child. Both her parents worked shifts and juggled childcare between them.

(Contd)

The problem
Ella had been dry since two years of age but refused to do a poo on the potty and insisted on wearing a nappy when she needed a poo.

The reason
With gentle questioning, her parents were able to find out why – she said she did not like it when the poo came away from her bottom.

The solution
Having understood the problem, we knew that Ella needed to be made to feel comfortable about letting go of her poo.

As always, with all problems with bowel training, we needed to be sure that constipation wasn't a contributing factor in the difficulty. So, before starting the plan we looked at Ella's diet to ensure that she was getting enough fibre and that she was drinking plenty of fluids. We also had a discussion about her poos to check that she was not suffering from constipation – fortunately, she was not.

The plan
WEEK ONE
- *Ella was allowed to wear her nappy whenever she needed a poo.*
- *Ella was encouraged to sit on the potty wearing the nappy when she did a poo.*
- *The potty had a wad of kitchen roll to fill up the space and to give padding under the nappy.*

INTERIM PROGRESS REPORT
After one week, Ella was happier sitting on the potty with a nappy on when she did a poo.

WEEK TWO
- *Ella's parents continued to place a wad of kitchen roll in the potty to fill up the space and to provide padding.*
- *Ella was encouraged to continue sitting on the potty with her nappy on, but this week the nappy was loosened around her tummy.*

THE OUTCOME OF WEEK TWO

From Day 1 to Day 4, Ella refused to sit on the potty without the nappy properly fastened. Each time she refused, the nappy was fastened back on and then she would sit on the potty.

On Day 5 Ella did sit on the potty with the nappy loosely fastened but then refused to do a poo, and the nappy needed to be firmly fastened before she would do a poo.

On Day 7 Ella sat on the potty with the nappy loosely fastened and did a poo.

WEEK THREE

Over the course of the next week the nappy was fastened a little more loosely each day, until by the end of Week three Ella was just sitting on the nappy, which was placed on top of the potty.

WEEK FOUR

The plan for Week four was that every time Ella needed to do a poo she was allowed to sit on the unfastened nappy with the kitchen roll for padding underneath. Each day a small section of the fresh nappy was cut away and the amount of kitchen roll reduced until, by the end of Week four, there was no more nappy or kitchen roll for Ella to sit on and she was doing her poo straight into the potty.

Her parents were advised not to rush her to use the toilet for doing a poo as the sound of the poo hitting the water in a toilet might well frighten her and set her back. Her parents agreed and waited three months before encouraging her to use the toilet, which she then did without an issue.

The outcome

Ella had a fear of letting go and that sense of the poo coming away and making a noise in the potty. This is a common issue with young children as the nappy offers secure padding to them.

(Contd)

The approach in Ella's case was in two steps (after identifying that she was not constipated). The first step was allowing her to continue doing a poo in her nappy but sitting on the potty with extra padding. The second step was to reduce the size of the nappy and the amount of padding under the nappy until there was no more nappy or padding. This took some time to achieve and her parents had to be very patient, but eventually, with a lot of patience and understanding, her parents achieved their goal.

Conclusion
In this case study, it is apparent that problems of this nature have a cause – and a solution. The important thing to remember is that quite often plenty of patience is required. If children have concerns about toilet training, they should not be rushed, as they need time to change their ideas and behaviour.

Frequently asked questions

Q1: *My daughter will only do a poo in her nappy although she is quite happy to do a wee on the potty. What can I do?*

This is a really common problem. First, let her continue to do the poo in her nappy but encourage her to sit on the potty with her nappy on. You may want to use a star chart. Once you have got her sitting on the potty with the nappy on to do the poo, the next step is to loosen the nappy until eventually she is sitting on the nappy (unfastened) with it on top of the potty. The final step is to reduce the size of the nappy. You can do this by cutting away a section of the nappy each time until there is no nappy left.

Q2: *My son is due to start school in a couple of months and my friend has told me that the teachers cannot help the children to wipe their bottoms. He has no idea how to and I always help him. I am really panicking about it.*

Young children often find this a difficult skill to master simply because their arms are not long enough. Your son needs plenty of practice before he starts school. So, every time he does a poo, give him the toilet paper and guide his hand to wipe his bottom. Keep practising and by the time he starts school he will be able to manage it for himself.

Q3: *My son's bowel habits are all over the place. One day he will do two poos and then it is maybe three or four days before the next one. Is this normal?*

Bowel habits differ from child to child but there are lots of ways to encourage a regular bowel habit. Firstly, make sure your child is drinking enough – at least six to eight small drinks, evenly spaced throughout the day. Look at the fibre content of your child's diet and get him into the habit of having a fibre-rich breakfast cereal, for example, porridge or Weetabix. Increase the amount of fresh fruit and vegetables. Make sure your son has plenty of time to sit on the toilet if he has the urge to do a poo and never rush him. Get into a routine of letting him sit on the toilet about 15 to 20 minutes after meals to see if he needs to do a poo. Once his bowel habits become more regular make sure you keep up the fluid and fibre content of his diet.

Summary

The key issue addressed in this chapter is the importance of treating and preventing constipation. With a little planning around eating habits, this issue can be very effectively dealt with. Constipation can be truly miserable for young children and if not treated can cause huge complications with toilet training. We've also seen how to get started on toilet training (bowels) and how we can ensure success in this area.

The next chapter deals with the very important issue of hand-washing and has a detailed section on everything you could possibly want to know about threadworms.

10 THINGS TO REMEMBER

1   *If your child suffers from constipation, this needs to be addressed before you start toilet training. Remember the signs to look out for to see if your child is constipated:*

    Fewer bowel movements than expected (less than three times per week).

    Pain and straining on passing stools.

    Tummy ache.

    Small, dry, hard stools.

    Avoiding the toilet.

    Not having an urge to do a poo.

    Feeling that a bowel movement isn't finished.

    Sore bottom.

2   *Treat constipation with an increase in dietary fibre and fluids.*

3   *To work out how much fibre your child needs, take her age in years and add five grams for children over two years. For example if your child is three years old, then the calculation would be 3 + 5 = 8 grams of fibre per day.*

4   *Remember, see your GP if your child is still suffering from constipation after you have increased fluids and fibre.*

5   *Childhood soiling is not that uncommon and is often caused by constipation.*

6   *Be prepared for accidents when you are getting started – it is a normal part of the toilet training process.*

7   *Keeping a diary can be very helpful in planning the process and is a good way to reflect on progress.*

8   *As soon as you decide to start toilet training do talk to your child about what is going to happen.*

9 *Remember to evaluate progress at the end of each day and reflect on how it has gone. This will help you to see if you need to make any changes.*

10 *If the training is not going well remember that it may be that your child is simply not ready. There is nothing wrong with putting a child back into nappies, leaving the training for a month and then trying again.*

6

Self-help skills

In this chapter you will learn:
- *why hand-washing is important*
- *how to help your child with personal hygiene*
- *everything you need to know about threadworms.*

Toilet training isn't just about your child being able to go to the toilet. There are many other important issues, one of which is the self-help skills that you need to make sure that your child develops in the coming months alongside the toilet training process. This chapter will help you to realize the importance of hand-washing and how you can get this message across to your child in a fun way. This chapter also addresses all those other hygiene issues – such as teaching your child how to wipe her bottom – and then finally there is an extensive section on everything you need to know about threadworms. You will find out just what they are, how to identify them, how to treat them and, most importantly, how to prevent your child getting them in the first place.

Hand-washing – why it is important

Hand-washing is the first line of defence against germs such as bacteria and viruses. These bacteria and viruses can be spread via:

- ▶ *dirty hands*
- ▶ *not washing hands after going to the toilet*

- *contaminated water and food*
- *a sick person's body fluids.*

If children pick up germs from one of these sources, they can unknowingly become infected simply by touching their eyes, nose or mouth, and once they are infected, it is only a matter of time before another family member or even the whole family comes down with the same illness. Good hand-washing is your first line of defence against the spread of a great many illnesses – and not just the common cold. The incidence of illnesses and conditions such as threadworms, meningitis, bronchiolitis, flu, hepatitis A and most types of infectious diarrhoea can be reduced by the simple act of washing your hands.

Insight

Hand-washing can reduce the spread of the common cold.

How to teach your child to wash her hands

The very best way to teach and encourage your child to wash her hands is to act as a role model, always washing your hands when you should. Being consistent about when she should wash her hands will ensure that your child becomes a regular hand-washer and help to reduce the possibility of your family being infected. In the early days, when you are teaching your child how to wash her hands, always do it with her to demonstrate just what you expect her to do. Then, when she has the hang of hand-washing always check that she has washed her hands thoroughly.

Here are the three simple steps to successfully scrubbing those germs away!

1 *Wash your child's hands in warm water, making sure the water is not too hot for little hands. Teach her which tap to turn on and how to turn it off. Make sure she knows how to tell the difference between the hot and the cold taps.*

2   *Use soap and lather up for about 20 seconds (antibacterial soap isn't necessary – any soap will do). Teach your child to wash between the fingers and under the nails where uninvited germs like to hang out (including threadworm eggs). And don't forget the wrists and backs of the hands.*
3   *Rinse and then dry well with a clean towel.*

Insight
Act as a role model. Make sure that you always wash your hands and that you do it properly. This is a life skill that you are teaching your child.

SOME IDEAS IF YOUR CHILD IS RELUCTANT ABOUT HAND-WASHING

Insight
▶ *Use colourful soaps made especially for children. Some soaps also come in interesting shapes or have fun scents to make hand-washing exciting.*
▶ *Sing a favourite song with your child while hand-washing. By the time the song is finished those germs will be washed away.*

To minimize the germs being passed around your family, have a clear set of family rules as to when everyone should wash their hands, especially:

▶ *before eating*
▶ *before cooking*
▶ *after going to the toilet*
▶ *after touching animals, including family pets*
▶ *after contact with sick friends or relatives*
▶ *after blowing your nose, coughing or sneezing*
▶ *after being outside (playing, gardening, walking the dog, etc.).*

Insight
One in three people do not wash their hands after going to the toilet.

Children need to have this routine instilled as part of their day by the time they go to nursery or school. It is not possible for staff to monitor children every time they go to the toilet to make sure they have washed their hands correctly, so make sure your child washes her hands properly as a matter of routine.

Personal hygiene

Teaching your child how to care for herself is an important life skill. It will help her in her journey towards independence. Children often find it quite difficult in the early days of toilet training to wipe themselves, especially after doing a poo, as their arms simply are not long enough. So, help your child to acquire this skill. NB: Little girls are obviously made differently so they need to learn to wipe from front to back to prevent poo from entering the urethra (the tube that leads to the bladder) as this could cause a urinary tract infection. Help your child to wipe herself by guiding her hand with the toilet paper. Encourage little boys to give their penis a little shake after a wee to get rid of any excess urine and to prevent damp patches on pants and trousers. The guideline is that by the time a child starts school, ideally she needs to be independent when it comes to toileting. In addition to being clean and dry throughout the day, this means being able to undress and dress as needed and to be able to wipe herself and then to know how to wash her hands properly. The only way to ensure this is to give her plenty of practice, so it is best to encourage the development of these self-help skills alongside the toilet training process and to continue practising them so that they become a part of daily life.

When children are first toilet training, a daily bath is a good idea, especially if they are a little accident-prone. Damp or soiled skin can get sore very quickly and a warm bath can be very soothing. It is also an ideal time to check your child for any signs of sore skin. When children are a little older and at school, where they are expected to sort themselves out in the toileting department, it is not uncommon for them to develop the odd bit of sore skin, so do be aware of that.

Lastly, daily fresh underpants or knickers are the order of the day. Again it is not uncommon when children are learning to wipe themselves for them to have soiled pants or knickers simply because they may be finding it a difficult skill to master and don't do the job quite as well as they should.

> **Insight**
> It is not uncommon when children first comes out of nappies for them to develop sore skin as they get to grips with cleaning themselves. Make sure that you help them and teach them how to wipe themselves after a poo.

Threadworms

WHAT ARE THREADWORMS?

Threadworms are small, white, thread-like worms between two and 13 mm long. They infect the human gut (intestines). They are common in children, but anyone of any age can be affected. They are often a cause of itchy bottoms and can cause other problems too, so threadworms must be sorted out if they occur in your family.

> **Insight**
> Threadworms are common but are not usually serious.

THE LIFE CYCLE OF THREADWORMS

If you need to eradicate threadworms in your family, it is useful to know a little about their life cycle. Threadworms live for about five to six weeks in the gut and then die. However, before they die the female worms lay tiny eggs around the anus (back passage) in both boys and girls, and around the vagina and urethra (this is the tube that carries urine from the bladder to the outside of the body) in girls. This usually happens at night when the infected child is asleep and warm. Threadworm eggs are not visible to the naked eye.

When laying the eggs, the female worm also secretes irritant mucus, which causes the child to scratch the itchy area. A child will often scratch the itchy area in their sleep without realizing. When a child scratches, eggs get onto the fingers and under fingernails and can then be swallowed when the child puts his hands in his mouth (as children often do). Threadworm eggs can survive for up to two weeks outside the body. They fall off the skin around the anus and can fall onto bedding, clothes, etc. They can also get wafted into the air as you change clothes and bedding and they become part of the house dust. Some eggs may settle on food and toothbrushes. Children may swallow some eggs at first by playing with other children who have eggs on their fingers, or from food, drink, toothbrushes or dust that has been contaminated with threadworm eggs. Parents often worry that family pets may pass on worms but threadworms only infest humans and cannot be caught from animals such as dogs and cats. However, there is a small risk that threadworms can be caught from household pets if their fur becomes contaminated with eggs as a result of human contact.

HOW CAN YOU TELL IF YOUR CHILD HAS THREADWORMS?

Threadworms can cause intense itching around the child's anus. Threadworms look like thin white cotton threads. Sometimes you can see them in the child's stool. If you cannot see the threadworm in the stool but suspect your child has threadworms (if they have been scratching their bottom, for example), try looking at the child's anus. You can do this with a torch in the late evening after your child has gone to sleep. Part your child's buttocks and look at the opening of the anus. If the child has threadworms, you can often see one or two coming out of their anus. DO NOT BE ALARMED! Either go and see your local pharmacist for advice on treatment or make an appointment with your GP. Treatments available today are very effective if used properly.

Threadworms can cause other symptoms, so you should keep an eye open for these. Some children find their sleep is disturbed because of the itching and discomfort. Large numbers of threadworms being present in the gut may possibly cause mild tummy pains and make a child irritable. In girls, threadworms can wander forwards and lay eggs in the vagina or urethra (the tube that passes urine). So, if your daughter has a vaginal discharge, is bedwetting after being dry at night or is having problems passing urine, do make an appointment with your GP, as threadworms may be the cause.

> **Insight**
> Threadworms do not always produce symptoms, therefore all family members should be treated even if only one person in the family has symptoms.

How do you treat threadworms?

Any attempt to eradicate threadworms from your family must be a two-pronged attack. You will need to:

- *use medication to get rid of the worms in the gut*
- *put in place hygiene measures to clear eggs which may be around the home to prevent re-infestation.*

Using one of these measures without the other will not give you a solution. Your measures also need to include everyone in the family.

MEDICATION

Medication can be bought from pharmacies to treat the worms in the gut or you can get medication on prescription from your GP. However, all members of the household need to be treated at the same time! This is vital.

> **Insight**
> If you are pregnant or breastfeeding do not take threadworm medication, but seek advice from your GP.

HYGIENE MEASURES

Medicine will kill the worms in the gut but will *not* affect the eggs that have been laid around the anus. These eggs can survive for up to two weeks outside the body – on underwear, bedding, in the house dust, etc. Hygiene measures aim to clear any eggs from the body and home, and also to prevent any eggs from being swallowed. This will break the cycle of re-infection. Every member of the household should do the following for two weeks after taking the first dose of medicine:

▶ *Wear underpants or knickers at night. This is so that if you scratch in your sleep, you will not touch the skin near the anus.*
▶ *Keep fingernails short.*
▶ *Discourage nail biting and thumb sucking.*
▶ *Wash hands and scrub nails every morning. Always wash hands before meals or snacks, before preparing food, after going to the toilet or changing a nappy or after touching the family pet.*
▶ *Every morning, have a bath/shower, or wash around the anus/ vagina (in girls) to get rid of any eggs laid overnight.*
▶ *Change and wash underwear, nightwear and bed linen – if possible every day. Avoid shaking clothes and linen as any eggs on them may be wafted into the air and become part of the dust.*
▶ *Wash cuddly toys.*
▶ *Make sure everyone has their own face flannel and towel to avoid using shared towels.*
▶ *Avoid eating food in the bedroom, as eggs can be present on bedclothes.*
▶ *Keep toothbrushes in a closed cupboard and rinse well before use.*

Also, on the day when you take the medicine, it is best to have a 'blitz' around the home, which aims to clear any eggs that may be part of the dust. This should include:

▶ *vacuuming and dusting all household carpets, particularly those where children play.*

- *damp-dusting smooth surfaces with a cloth rinsed in hot water. Again, concentrate on places where children play, and in bedrooms and the bathroom. Throw out the cloth after use.*

What about my child going to nursery or school?

There is no need to keep a child with threadworms off nursery or school. The hygiene measures described above will mean that your child will not have any eggs on their fingers when they go out from the home each day and so cannot infect others. However, it is a good idea to let the nursery or school know that your child has threadworms as they may well have picked it up there.

There is a useful organization called the **Threadworm Action Panel**, which holds a Threadworm Action Week each year to raise the awareness of the issue of threadworms. Your child's nursery or school may be interested in receiving a Threadworm fact pack and promoting awareness of the issue. They have a website at www.fredworm.co.uk.

Frequently asked questions

Q1: *We have had a note home from school to say that there has been an outbreak of threadworms at school. I am not sure how I can prevent my two children from getting them. Can you help?*

Threadworms are very common and are usually harmless. To prevent your children from becoming infected make sure they know how to wash their hands properly. By this we mean using warm water with soap and washing their hands, between fingers and backs of hands for a good 20 seconds. Go through with them when it is important to wash hands – so, always after going to the toilet, before eating food, after touching any animal or playing outside. Once a week check their nails. Keep nails short as threadworm eggs can get caught under nails and then ingested. If your child bites her nails, try to discourage her from doing so.

Q2: *I know how important it is for children to wash their hands but my son just seems to forget all the time. What can I do?*

Your son needs you and other family members to be his role models. So every time he is in the bathroom let him see you and other family members washing their hands. When he has been to the toilet or there is a need for him to wash his hands, do it with him to reinforce the message. Make it fun, sing a song together while he is washing and have a look for the children's liquid soaps on the market. If he has his own special soap it may well encourage him to wash his hands.

Summary

This chapter has focused on the self-help skills that children need to develop to complete the toilet training journey, such as wiping their bottoms and hand-washing. The best way to develop these skills is for them to learn hand-in-hand with the skills of toilet training.

The chapter has also detailed all the information that a family needs to avoid infestation with threadworms or, if infested, to deal with the issue effectively.

10 THINGS TO REMEMBER

1 *Hand-washing is a really important skill for a child to learn.*

2 *Always wash hands before eating or cooking and after going to the toilet, touching animals (including family pets), contact with sick friends or relatives, blowing your nose, coughing or sneezing or after being outside.*

3 *The best way to teach your child to wash her hands well is to act as a role model.*

4 *If your child is a reluctant hand-washer remember that there are ways to encourage a good hand-washing routine, e.g. colourful soaps or a star chart.*

5 *Remember that children need to be helped with personal hygiene and taught the best way to keep clean, e.g. teaching little girls to wipe from front to back.*

6 *A daily change of underwear is a must.*

7 *Look out for signs of threadworms – sometimes they can be seen in your child's poo or you may notice that she is scratching her bottom.*

8 *Threadworms are easily treated but remember that all the family must be treated at the same time.*

9 *If you are pregnant, see your GP for advice about treatment for threadworms.*

10 *You do not need to keep your child at home from nursery or playgroup if she has threadworms.*

7

Common problems

In this chapter you will learn:
- *about the most common problems that occur when toilet training*
- *strategies for how to deal with them*
- *about real-life examples of how these problems can be tackled.*

If you have turned to this chapter, you have most likely started the toilet training process and have encountered difficulties. Toilet training can be fraught with dilemmas and plenty of hassle if either you or your child is not ready. If you have not already read Chapter 2 on toilet readiness and completed the 'Toilet readiness questionnaire', then this is the time to do it. Many toilet training issues are caused by the child simply not being ready and by parents expecting too much too soon. So, if you are encountering difficulties, reassess the situation. Do the questionnaire and check if your child really is ready. If you are totally convinced that your child is ready but you are having to deal with a specific problem that is hampering your progress in toilet training your child, then maybe you will find the answer to your dilemma in this chapter of case studies.

Insight
If you are struggling to work out why training is not going well, keep a diary. This can be a real eye opener as to what the issue may be.

Each of the case studies in this chapter is designed to illustrate the effects of some of these common problems and, most importantly, to show you, in detail, how they can be solved.

Wetting or having lots of accidents

Frequent wetting is a common problem and very frustrating for the parents as it leads to lots of extra washing. The most patient of parents may well begin to get cross and grumpy, but that will not help the situation at all. Here is a checklist of reasons why frequent wetting may be occurring:

▶ *Your child does not have toilet readiness; there may well be specific areas where your child needs to fine-tune the skills needed. Complete the 'Toilet readiness questionnaire' in Chapter 2 and identify the areas that need developing, then turn to Chapter 3 for ideas on developing these missing skills.*

▶ *Your child tends to get easily distracted by what they are doing and forgets that he needs to go on the potty, or is so absorbed in what he is doing that he delays going until it is too late. This is a very common problem and there are a number of strategies that can be put in place to help overcome the issues.*

▶ *Your child simply may not be having enough fluids on a regular basis throughout the day. When a child does not have adequate fluids, the urine becomes concentrated. Concentrated urine can irritate the bladder and cause wetting, so make sure your child is having at least six to eight drinks (150 ml each drink) of, ideally, water or milk at regular intervals throughout the day.*

▶ *Your child is suffering from constipation. Having a full bowel can press on the bladder and give the urge to urinate frequently. Read Chapter 5, which has an extensive section on constipation and diet. You may need to pay special attention to your child's diet but if the problem is not improving, then a visit to your GP may be required.*

- ▶ *Your child may have a urinary tract infection. Read Chapter 11, which has a section on urinary tract infections. If you suspect a urinary tract infection your child will need to see your GP.*
- ▶ *Your child may be having fluids that encourage him to pass urine very frequently. These include any drinks with caffeine in, hot chocolate, fizzy drinks and fruit juices, especially blackcurrant.*

Insight

If your child is having lots of accidents when you first start toilet training, go back and re-do the toilet readiness questionnaire. Has your child got all the necessary skills in place?

Case study

Rhianna (two years and seven months) was the first child in her family. Her father worked full time and her mother part time. Rhianna attended nursery in the mornings from 8 a.m. to 1 p.m. She had not worn nappies since the age of two years and three months but had continued to have frequent accidents. She was a very busy, bright child who was also a poor sleeper.

The problem

Rhianna often had to be woken up in the morning in time to go to nursery as she tended to settle quite late at night, and also it was not uncommon for her to be up three or four times during the night. Rhianna, understandably, was quite grumpy on waking and often resisted getting out of bed. This gave quite a stressful start to the day for both Rhianna and her parents. However, by the time she arrived at nursery, Rhianna was usually in a better frame of mind and she enjoyed her session each morning. During the course of the morning she usually managed to be accident free. The nursery that Rhianna attended had a high staff ratio and was well structured, with toileting routines in place. During the week at nursery Rhianna tended to have one to two accidents over the

(Contd)

course of the week. When Rhianna was collected from nursery at 1 p.m. she was clearly beginning to feel very tired after her busy morning, but nevertheless she resisted an afternoon nap. She would invariably have an accident soon after arriving home. Quite often she would fall asleep at about 4 p.m. while watching a video. Rhianna's mother would then let her sleep until 6 p.m. when Rhianna would be woken for her tea. The evening would again be stressful with one or two accidents and eventually Rhianna's parents would get her to bed between 9.30 and 10 p.m.

The reason
Rhianna was a very tired little girl and her tiredness was impacting on the toilet training. She was also a very busy child who needed a structured routine to remind her of the need to go to the toilet.

The solution
Before implementing a programme for Rhianna, we first needed to assess the three following areas.

1. DID RHIANNA HAVE TOILET READINESS?

We completed the 'Toilet readiness questionnaire' (see Chapter 2) and she had a high score. Rhianna had also demonstrated that in a structured environment with a routine in place she had very few accidents.

2. WAS RHIANNA SUFFERING FROM CONSTIPATION?

This was assessed and she was found not to have constipation but to have a balanced, varied diet with a reasonable amount of fibre and a good fluid intake. She had her bowels open once or twice a day and the stools were of normal appearance.

3. DID RHIANNA HAVE A URINARY TRACT INFECTION?

Rhianna's mother had already taken Rhianna to the GP and her urine had been tested and it was negative. She showed no physical signs of a urinary tract infection (see Chapter 11). Also, she was usually fine all morning at nursery, so this also suggested that there were no medical problems to be addressed.

The plan
1 *The first issue – Rhianna needed to have a more structured routine surrounding sleep to combat the tiredness that was affecting her toilet training.*
2 *The second issue – the wetting. Rhianna needed a toileting routine at home similar to that in place at nursery.*

WEEK ONE

Sleep

Rhianna's mother agreed that on returning home from nursery, Rhianna needed a period of quiet time. Rhianna loved books and was just getting interested in story tapes.

The following routine was suggested:

1 *On arrival home, Rhianna would be taken to the toilet and encouraged to do a wee. It did not matter if she did not do one, but she was to be praised for sitting on the toilet.*
2 *Then a nappy was put on and she was settled down in bed, with the curtains drawn.*
3 *Her mother would read two short stories that Rhianna could choose and would then put on a story tape of her favourite book character 'Alfie'.*
4 *Her mother would leave the room on the understanding with Rhianna that this was her quiet time. Rhianna was to stay in bed until the story tape had finished.*

Toileting
1 *Rhianna was to be taken to the toilet as soon as she arrived home.*
2 *When she went for her quiet time in bed, a nappy was to be put on.*
3 *On getting up, the nappy was to be taken off and Rhianna taken to the toilet.*

(Contd)

4   *After that, Rhianna's mother was to firmly, but gently, take Rhianna to the toilet every one and a half hours until bedtime. If Rhianna was busy with a toy or game, her mother needed to reassure her that the toy or game would still be there on her return.*

Bedtime

1   *A firm bedtime routine needed to be established. Rhianna's usual bedtime was between 9.30 and 10 p.m. This was too late for her, as it did not give sufficient time for her to get the amount of sleep she needed and would also mean that she was over-tired when she got to bed. Due to being over-tired she found it very difficult to settle and then woke frequently. The new bedtime routine was to consist of:*

6 p.m.	*Tea*
6.30–7.30 p.m.	*Play, but no television or videos so that Rhianna could wind down*
7.30 p.m.	*Bath and fresh nappy*
8 p.m.	*Milk and clean teeth*
8.10 p.m.	*Two stories chosen by Rhianna and then a story tape*

2   *If Rhianna woke during the night (which she tended to do up to three to four times per night), her parents were to take her back to bed and quietly settle her down. (Her parents usually let her get into their bed after they had been disturbed three or four times).*

Rhianna's mother knew it was going to be a difficult, tiring week as there were two issues that were going to be addressed in one go – the wetting and the sleeping.

DAY 1

An amazing thing happened on the first day of the routine. Rhianna was taken to the toilet on arriving home (she did not do anything) and then went to bed with her two stories that she had chosen. Her mother left her listening to the story tape as agreed. After about 20 minutes she went to check on Rhianna and found that she was fast asleep. It had been agreed if Rhianna did fall asleep, she should not be allowed to sleep for any more than two hours. Rhianna's mother woke her up at 3.30 p.m. Her nappy was wet but she also did a wee on the toilet as well. Rhianna was then taken to the toilet again at 5 p.m. and at 6.30 p.m. On both occasions she did a wee on the toilet.

The evening routine was instigated as recommended. Rhianna was settled in bed shortly after 8 p.m. with her two short stories and was then left with the story tape. Rhianna was reluctant to settle and got up twice, but was taken straight back to bed. By 9 p.m. she was asleep. Rhianna woke twice during the night but her parents persuaded her to go back to bed, and they resettled her each time.

DAY 2
On arrival home, Rhianna did a wee on the toilet and then settled down in bed with her two stories and the story tape. She was asleep by 1.30 p.m. and woke with a dry nappy. Rhianna had a friend round to play and she stayed for tea. Because Rhianna's mother was distracted making tea for Rhianna and her little friend and chatting to the friend's mum, she forgot to take Rhianna to the toilet, with the consequence that Rhianna wet herself at 5.15 p.m.

The evening routine went well and Rhianna was again settled in bed shortly after 8 p.m. She needed to be resettled only once and was asleep by 8.40 p.m. Rhianna woke three times again during the night but was quickly and quietly resettled each time.

DAY 3
There was success on the toilet on arrival home and Rhianna slept for two hours and then woke with a dry nappy. Rhianna's mother was more careful today to remember to take Rhianna to the toilet every one and a half hours and there were no accidents.

(Contd)

Rhianna was in bed shortly after 8 p.m. and only needed to be resettled once and was asleep by 8.30 p.m. She woke twice during the night and was quickly resettled.

INTERIM PROGRESS REPORT

Rhianna's parents were delighted and surprised at the progress that Rhianna had made in what felt like a very short space of time. Rhianna had very clearly responded to the routine and the security that it gave her. She was now having that much-needed sleep at an appropriate time in the afternoon and had also had a bedtime routine established. She also had a routine established at home for toileting, with visits to the toilet every one and a half hours. Rhianna was the sort of child who got very absorbed in what she was doing or playing with, so it was essential that she was reminded to go to the toilet. When these reminders were given she remained dry, which is what happened at nursery.

Her parents were a little concerned about the need to resettle her at night but were reassured that if they continued to resettle her with the minimum of fuss she would stop waking.

DAYS 4 TO 7

Progress continued to be made and by the end of the first week Rhianna was having a two-hour sleep on arriving home and would wake with a dry nappy. As long as her mother remembered to take her to the toilet every one and a half hours, she remained accident free.

In the evenings she was settling by 8.30 p.m. and by the end of the week did not need to be resettled in the evening. She did, however, continue to wake at night, but this had reduced to twice a night.

WEEK TWO

The plan for this week was to encourage Rhianna to take some initiative in deciding when she needed to do a wee, rather than having to be taken. Also, now that an evening routine had been established, her parents could bring the routine forward so that Rhianna would be settled and asleep by 7.30 p.m. each evening.

DAYS 1, 2 AND 3

1 *Rhianna's mother was asked to stop Rhianna doing whatever it was she was doing and to ask her if she needed to go to the toilet (instead of taking Rhianna to the toilet every one and a half hours). If Rhianna said yes then she would take her but if she said no then she could leave her to play.*

2 *In the event of Rhianna having an accident, Rhianna's mother was to discuss with her what it felt like to need a wee.*

Tea was brought forward to 5.30 p.m. and bath time to 7 p.m. with a view to Rhianna being settled between 7.45 and 8 p.m.

INTERIM PROGRESS REPORT

Day 1

There was one accident just before teatime. Rhianna had said she did not need a wee and then 15 minutes later had had an accident. When they had a chat about it, Rhianna admitted that she was enjoying her game and did not want to go to the toilet because she wanted to continue playing. Her mother reinforced that it would be OK for Rhianna to go to the toilet and her game would not be disturbed.

An earlier tea worked a treat and Rhianna was in bed and asleep by 7.45 p.m. She woke only once during the night.

Days 2 and 3

On both days Rhianna did a wee when she was asked if she needed one and no accidents happened.

Both evenings Rhianna was settled by 7.45 p.m. and slept through to the morning. (This was the first time she had slept all night since birth.)

Days 4 to 7

It was agreed that Rhianna had made great progress and was now pretty much dry throughout the day although she still needed, on occasion, to be asked if she needed to go to the toilet.

(Contd)

Teatime was brought forward to 5 p.m. with a bath at 6 p.m.
Bedtime was moved to shortly after 7 p.m.

The outcome
Now that Rhianna was a much more rested little girl who was
sleeping 11 to 12 hours a night and two hours in the afternoon,
she was much more even-tempered. The idea of her making the
decision about if she needed to go to the toilet appealed to her and,
now that she was not over-tired and was generally calmer, it was
almost as if she was able to think more clearly about what was
going on. The technique worked and, apart from an accident on
Day 5, by the end of the second week she was accident free.

The earlier tea/bath routine worked and she was asleep
by 7.30 p.m. and was sleeping through.

Conclusion
Toilet training can often be influenced by other factors that appear
to bear no relation to toileting.

Rhianna had toilet readiness and the physical skills in place, but
because of her poor sleep pattern she needed the constant prompt
of being reminded to go (and, of course, this is what happened at
nursery). Without the prompt it was all too much for her to manage.
She was over-tired and this showed itself in her grumpy behaviour and
her 'busy, busy' personality. Rhianna needed to have her sleep issues
addressed as they were impacting on her ability to stay dry. She was
also a very 'busy' child who became very absorbed in what she was
doing. She needed the reassurance that her game would still be there
if she needed to go to the toilet. Also, by ensuring that she went to the
toilet on a regular basis, it helped to improve her bladder tone and
for her to identify when her bladder was full and needed emptying.

> **Insight**
> Once you have got a routine established, get your child used
> to making the decision when he needs to go to the toilet,
> instead of him depending on you to remind him. He needs to
> be able to listen to his own body cues.

Checklist if your child is wetting

If frequent accidents are a problem for you and your child, go through this list and see which scenarios apply to your child:

- ▶ *Is your child going to the toilet often enough? Encourage him to empty his bladder every two hours at least. This will improve the muscle tone of the bladder and will then help your child to recognize when his bladder is full and needs emptying. Do make sure your child is drinking enough.*
- ▶ *If your child gets very involved with what he is doing, begin by firmly but gently taking him to the toilet every one and a half hours. Again, this will help him to improve the muscle tone of the bladder and will increase awareness of when the bladder is full. Always reassure your child that his game will still be there when he returns. Once you have established that routine, the next step is to ask him if he needs the toilet. Make sure when you are asking him that you have eye contact with him and that he has heard what you have said. At this stage your aim is for him to begin to identify for himself that his bladder is full and that it needs emptying.*
- ▶ *There may be an issue that needs medical attention. Read the sections on constipation (Chapter 5) and urinary tract infections (Chapter 11) and follow the advice offered.*
- ▶ *Check what your child is drinking. There may well be certain fluids that he is having that are making him wee more than he should do. As stated previously, the ideal drinks for young children are milk and water.*

The problem of soiling

WHAT IS SOILING?

Stool soiling – also called encopresis – happens when children who are already toilet trained accidentally leak faeces onto their pants. Stool soiling most often occurs as a result of constipation.

Most often the amount of soiling is small and just stains the
underwear. In almost all cases, stool soiling is involuntary, which
means that your child has no control over it. This can seem strange
to parents so a little explanation of the situation is called for.
This is what often happens:

▶ *The child has a hard stool. This may follow an illness, and
it hurts when he passes it. Occasionally, there may even be a
small tear in the skin around the anus caused by passing large,
hard stools and there may also be a small amount of blood.
The child then, understandably, tries to hold on to his poo to
stop it from hurting.*
▶ *Sometimes the pain makes the muscle where the poo comes
out tighten up and this makes it even harder to poo.*
▶ *The poo then gets bigger and harder and stretches the walls of
the bowel. This makes it harder for the child to feel just when
it is time to go to the toilet, as he does not know if the bowel
is full.*
▶ *In the end, sometimes the softer poo from above the hard,
large poo leaks around the edges and soils the pants.*

Any child who is soiling needs to be seen by the GP. Treatment
can be:

1 *medication prescribed by your doctor to soften the stool*
2 *diet to include an increased amount of fibre and also an
increase in fluid intake*
3 *retraining to use the toilet.*

STEPS TO HELP DEAL WITH SOILING

▶ If your child is suffering from constipation he will need to see your family doctor for medication. It is important that you continue with the medication even after the constipation has cleared to help retrain your child's bowel.

▶ Make sure your child is getting enough fluids to drink. Remember: six to eight small drinks at regular intervals throughout the day.

▶ Providing a balanced diet that is rich in fibre is essential.

▶ Make sure your child knows what it feels like to have a full bowel; this will encourage him to know when to go to the toilet.

▶ Help your child to feel happy about going to the toilet; do not rush him and check that he feels comfortable about using the potty or toilet.

▶ Get into a regular routine of encouraging your child to sit on the potty or toilet 15–20 minutes after a meal.

▶ If using the toilet, a small step for your child to rest his feet on will help him to be in the correct position to empty his bowel fully.

▶ Plenty of exercise promotes healthy bowel activity.

▶ Don't forget lots of praise.

▶ If your child does soil, just clean him up and try not to make a fuss; remember, it is not his fault that this is happening.

Insight

Once constipation is under control, make sure you keep up the fibre content and the extra fluids to prevent it happening again.

Stress-related soiling

Soiling accidents can sometimes occur in children when they have just started school or if they are unhappy or under pressure. This can occur months and even years after achieving full bowel control and with no associated physical problem such as constipation. This can cause huge embarrassment and upset for the child and family trying to cope in this situation. It is always important as a first step with any soiling to check if the child is suffering from constipation. If this is not the case then trying to find the source of the child's unhappiness or anxiety is the next step. The school nurse and family doctor may suggest an assessment from a clinical psychologist. Discovering the cause of the unhappiness or anxiety will allow the family to help the child resolve the issues.

Case study

Peter (three years and nine months) was the fourth child in the family. All the older siblings were at school full-time and Peter attended the local nursery (mornings only) that was attached to the primary school where his siblings were pupils.

The problem
Peter had been toilet trained by the age of three years. The soiling had started in the last four months following a nasty tummy upset. Peter had his bowels open once a day but there was often soiling on his pants when he went to do a wee. Children at the nursery were beginning to comment and had made unkind remarks about him. Peter was beginning to feel very self-conscious about the soiling and had recently started to say that he did not want to go to nursery any more. Peter's mother had never encountered soiling with her older three children and was really at a loss as to what was causing it and how to remedy the situation.

The reason
Peter had developed severe constipation following a stomach upset and the constipation had resulted in soiling.

The solution
Peter had suffered a very nasty tummy bug and the soiling had started soon after that. Although Peter did go to the toilet every day, some days his stools were quite hard and pellet-like and some days they were very liquid. Peter also complained of stomach ache from time to time. After a detailed discussion as to his bowel habits and a look at his diet, it was suspected that he was constipated. Peter was taken to his GP who confirmed this suspicion and prescribed a course of stool-softening medicine. It was agreed that alongside the

stool-softening medicine, Peter's diet needed an overhaul. Peter's mother was advised that the stool-softening medicine should be given at night-time and that once Peter was pooing on a regular basis and the poo was soft and easy to pass, the dose could be reduced. The GP thought it would take a couple of months of medication to sort out the problem. The change in diet needed to be quite gradual so as not to cause any unpleasant side-effects such as wind and bloating.

Peter's typical daily diet at this point was:

Breakfast:
Rice Krispies with semi-skimmed milk and half a banana
Apple juice

Mid-morning at nursery:
Half an apple cut up
Drink of water

Lunch:
Cheese sandwich made with white bread
1 pot of full-fat yoghurt
Apple juice

Mid-afternoon:
1 packet of crisps
Drink of milk

Dinner:
2 sausages and mashed potato with a very small portion of carrots
Ice cream
Apple juice

It was agreed that the following changes needed to be made to Peter's diet to increase the fibre content and to give him more fluids:

▶ *Increase fluid intake to eight small drinks each day instead of five.*
▶ *Apple juice should only be given once a day and this should be diluted.*

(Contd)

- ▶ It was agreed that Peter would be offered either water or milk at other times.
- ▶ Peter was allowed to choose a water bottle with his favourite character on to encourage him to drink more.
- ▶ An alternative breakfast cereal needed to be introduced to increase the fibre content of his diet. Rice Krispies have a very low fibre rating. It was suggested that porridge and Weetabix would increase the fibre content of his diet.
- ▶ Peter needed to increase his intake of fruit and vegetables.
- ▶ Replacing the white bread with wholemeal bread was suggested.
- ▶ The mid-afternoon snack of crisps was to be replaced with dried fruit.

Week one

DIET AND FLUIDS

There would be a lot of dietary changes to cope with, so we decided that the first week's changes would focus on increasing Peter's fluid intake and changing his breakfast cereal, plus introducing more fruit. The cereals suggested were porridge and Weetabix as these are excellent sources of soluble fibre. Peter's mother was not convinced that Peter would agree to these changes. Peter liked yoghurt so it was decided that a small pot of yoghurt would be added to the porridge once it had been made with milk or poured over the Weetabix. A fruit platter was introduced after lunch and dinner. On a plate, a small selection of three fruits was offered to encourage Peter to eat more fruit and also a wider variety. Peter's fluid intake was increased to eight drinks each day. The apple juice was offered only once a day and milk and water were offered at other times.

TOILETING

Peter was to be encouraged to sit on the toilet after each meal to see if he needed a poo. He was also brought a small step to rest his feet on when sitting on the toilet.

MEDICATION

Peter took the medication each evening as prescribed by the GP.

INTERIM PROGRESS REPORT

Diet and fluids

Much to his mother's surprise, Peter really liked the porridge and the Weetabix mixed with yoghurt. By the end of the week he was asking for the 'yoghurt cereal'. The idea of the fruit platter took a few days to get off the ground, but his older siblings were also encouraged to join in with the idea. The agreement was that all the fruit was to be eaten before any pudding was given. Increasing Peter's fluid intake proved easy, he just needed to be reminded to keep drinking.

Toileting and medication

Peter was happy to sit on the toilet and by the end of the week he was having two poos a day. Some of the poos were still quite firm but the medication was working its magic.

Week two

DIET

The plan this week was to introduce dried fruit as a mid-afternoon snack, substitute wholemeal bread for white bread at lunchtime and to encourage Peter to eat more vegetables. Peter was not keen on dried fruit, but yoghurt-dipped dried fruit did appeal to him. Peter refused point-blank to eat wholemeal bread but then his older brother came up with the idea of wholemeal pitta bread, which Peter did like. The suggestion with the vegetables was that Peter was to be given two very small portions of vegetables at lunchtime and at dinnertime. If he did not eat them, no comment would be made, but if he did, lots of praise would be given.

INTERIM PROGRESS REPORT

Diet and fluids

The yoghurt-dipped fruit and wholemeal pitta bread were both a great success. The extra vegetables were not as successful. However, Peter's mother was reminded that children needed to be exposed to a new food up to 17 times before they will even try it. So she was encouraged to keep offering an assortment of vegetables, as it was still early days in the drive to transform Peter's diet. Peter's fluid intake had increased and he was now even asking for extra drinks.

(Contd)

Toileting and medication

Peter continued with the medication nightly. He was now pooing twice a day and was asking to go as soon as he had the urge to empty his bowels. His stools were much softer and the soiling was becoming less frequent.

The outcome

Peter continued on his stool-softening medicine for another two weeks. He was taken to see the GP who suggested reducing the dose by half for two more weeks and then stopping the medication. By the end of the fourth week, Peter was pooing twice a day. The stools were soft and well formed and the soiling had stopped. Peter was doing well with all the dietary changes and his mother was continuing to encourage him with the vegetables.

Conclusion

This case study is another example of a situation where other influences can affect toilet training. In this case it was an illness and its after-effects. It demonstrates the importance of taking an overall, holistic view of the situation and shows how putting really quite simple measures in place can result in a situation being dramatically turned around.

Checklist if your child is soiling

▶ *If a child is soiling he should always, in the first instance, be seen by his GP.*

▶ *An overhaul of the child's diet and fluid intake needs to be done. As the vast majority of cases of soiling are due to constipation, dietary changes will need to be made. A referral to a dietician may be recommended.*

▶ *Once dietary changes are made it is crucial that these changes are kept up, otherwise the problem will just come back at a later date.*

▶ *If medication is prescribed, again it is important that the medication is taken as directed.*

▶ *Measures should be put in place to ensure the child feels comfortable about doing a poo. If he is using a toilet, is there a step for him to rest his feet on? Does he have privacy when he needs to do a poo? Is he given enough time and not hurried. If they have experienced a hard dry stool that has hurt, children can become afraid of doing a poo on the toilet for fear that it will hurt. For a short period of time they may need to be allowed to do a poo in their nappy. This serves two purposes. The first is that it gives them back a sense of security and the second is that they may find it more comfortable when pushing out the poo, to be able to push against the nappy.*

Refusing to sit on the potty

Another common problem encountered when toilet training is that children often refuse to sit on the potty. This can cause immense frustration for a parent, but as we have said before, the only person who has control in the toilet training process is your child. You therefore need to work with your child to try and find out the reason why he is refusing to sit on the potty. This may be something very simple, ranging from the fact he doesn't like the colour of the potty to a case of too much pressure being put on him to sit on it.

Of course, there will be occasions when a parent will not be able to work out why the child has a problem with the potty and then they just need to find a solution acceptable to both the parent and the child. This can often be going straight to using the toilet and bypassing the use of the potty.

Let's look at an example of this sort of problem:

Case study

Hannah (two years and ten months) was a twin – her identical twin sister was Beatrice. Beatrice had been toilet trained since the age
(Contd)

of two years and six months but Hannah showed no interest, and refused to sit on a potty. The girls' mother had been keen to get them both out of nappies at the same time but her plan had failed to work. Their mother had been surprised at what had happened. She had assumed that Hannah would have been potty trained first, as she had always reached a new milestone before her sister.

The problem
Hannah showed absolutely no interest whatsoever in toilet training – to the extent that when her twin sister sat on the potty to do a wee or a poo, Hannah would either turn her back on her or walk out of the room. Hannah's mother was very puzzled by this behaviour. On further discussion, it materialized that when Hannah's mother had started to train the girls at the same time she had inadvertently put more pressure on Hannah. She had assumed that Hannah would have no problem with toilet training as in the past she had always done things before her sister. In contrast, she had not really put much pressure on Beatrice, not expecting her to do it quickly. Because there had been no pressure on Beatrice to perform, she had quietly got on with the job in hand and trained within a few days. The expectation of easy success had had an adverse effect on Hannah.

The reason
Too much pressure had been put on Hannah to train and she had completely switched off from the idea.

The solution
1 *The girls' parents needed to start treating them as individuals in their own right and stop comparing them. This is, of course, a common problem with twins and it needs a conscious effort not to make too many assumptions and to ensure even-handedness.*
2 *Beatrice received lots of attention when she used the potty, which was having a negative effect on Hannah. This needed to be turned around.*
3 *It was felt that, as Hannah had such a negative view of the potty, it would be best to miss out the potty stage and move straight to the toilet.*

WEEK ONE

1 *A star chart was to be introduced for the girls. Each child would have their own chart, which they would help to decorate. They were allowed to choose their own stickers. (Hannah chose kittens and Beatrice chose frogs.)*

2 *Each child had three tasks on their chart, which were different. Hannah had brushing teeth, putting on her shoes and helping to lay the table for meals. Beatrice had hand-washing, putting on her socks and helping clear away after meals.*

3 *The parents were encouraged to make sure that the children received, as far as possible, an equal amount of praise and stickers.*

4 *It was agreed that the potty would stay in the bathroom rather than the main room that the girls were playing in. If Hannah happened to be in the bathroom when Beatrice used the potty, Beatrice would be quietly praised rather than a big fuss being made.*

5 *Toilet training was not discussed with Hannah during the week.*

INTERIM PROGRESS REPORT

The first week progressed really well. Hannah and Beatrice loved the star charts and were very excited whenever they got a sticker. Much to their mother's surprise, they also seemed to really like the idea that they both got stickers for different reasons. Now came the tricky bit – we needed to work out a way of encouraging Hannah to sit on a toilet seat. It was suggested that Hannah and Beatrice were taken shopping. Beatrice needed a new drinking beaker as the lid of hers was broken and Hannah was allowed to choose a child's toilet seat. However, she did not look too impressed until her mother told her that some children like to be different and not use a potty but to go straight to using a toilet seat. This appealed to Hannah. It was agreed that on Beatrice's chart a new target was added: sitting on the potty. Of course, this was very easy for Beatrice and she would get extra stickers over the course of each day. On Hannah's chart we added sitting on the toilet seat. Hannah's mother was quick to reassure Hannah that all she had to do was sit on the toilet seat and she could do it wearing her clothes if she wanted.

(Contd)

On Days 1 and 2 Hannah showed no inclination to sit on the toilet seat. But by the end of Day 2 it was obvious to Hannah that Beatrice had more stickers. On the morning of Day 3, after getting dressed, Hannah announced that she would sit on the toilet seat. She did so and lots of fuss was made, with even Beatrice getting excited for her. As the week progressed Hannah sat on the toilet seat with her clothes on, three or four times a day. By the end of the week she was tending to do it each time that she realized that Beatrice had used the potty. So a pattern was developing.

WEEK THREE
The target was changed to Hannah sitting on the toilet seat with a nappy on. Hannah was happy to accept this and the week went well. The pattern had now become established that when Beatrice would go to use the potty in the bathroom, Hannah would follow and sit on the toilet seat and then they would both get their stickers.

WEEK FOUR
Again the target was changed – this time to Hannah sitting on the toilet seat with no nappy. There was no resistance at all.

The outcome
By the middle of Week four, Hannah was not only sitting on the toilet seat but she was doing a wee as well. By the end of Week five she was dry and clean. Hannah had just wanted to be given her own space to acquire the skills and also to be allowed to be different.

Conclusion
Twins should always be treated as individuals and allowed to develop at their own personal rate. Look at each child's readiness and proceed accordingly.

Checklist if your child does not want to sit on a potty

So, what should you do if you encounter this problem with your child? Try these suggestions:

- See if you can figure out why your child is not keen. There may be a really simple reason such as:
  - they don't like the colour of the potty
  - they don't feel comfortable
  - they may want a bit more privacy
  - they may feel that sitting on a potty is babyish
  - you may have inadvertently put them off by putting too much pressure on them.
- Sticker charts can often work a treat in this situation, but do it slowly. Introduce the sticker chart for other targets first, then add sitting on the potty. Break this down into the different stages – sitting on the potty with a nappy on and clothes, then just a nappy and finally without a nappy.
- Remember don't put pressure on your child; it will only backfire and it will take longer to train.
- Some children really cannot be doing with the potty – just let them use the toilet!

If your child is hiding when doing a poo

The most likely explanation for this situation is that they are at a point in their very young lives when, for some reason, they need control over what is happening to them. Doing a poo where you are not supposed to is a sure-fire way of getting attention, and at this point they need this attention for whatever reason. Read the following case study of how a little boy was reacting to his sister going to school.

Case study

Joshua (three years and four months) was the second child in the family. He had an older sister who was five years old and who had already started school full-time. Joshua went to a private nursery three days a week while his mother worked. Joshua and Melissa (his sister) had been at the same nursery together until she had started school.

(Contd)

The problem
Joshua had started hiding when doing a poo and doing the poo in his pants. This had coincided with Melissa leaving the nursery and starting school. There were no issues about passing urine, which he happily did in the toilet at home, and at nursery.

The reason
Joshua was missing his sibling and he was communicating his loss by pooing in his pants.

The plan
Joshua was clearly missing his sister a great deal. Joshua had attended the nursery from six months of age and was used to Melissa always being there. They went to nursery only three days a week and so on the other days at home he had also had Melissa there. Joshua was finding life without Melissa difficult to cope with.

Joshua's parents went into the nursery and had a meeting with his key worker. It became apparent that Joshua had been extremely attached to Melissa while they were at nursery together and Joshua had not taken a huge amount of interest in the other children, as he had a ready-made playmate, of course. His key worker described him as being quite a solitary child who now appeared happy with his own company. Joshua was hiding and pooing in his pants both at nursery and at home, although, interestingly, he was less likely to do it at weekends when Melissa was there.

The nursery agreed that they needed to encourage Joshua to socialize and interact more with the other children. There were two children at the nursery with whom Joshua had shown some interest in playing. It was decided that the nursery would encourage some small group activities, which would include Joshua and these two children in an attempt to encourage Joshua to socialize. Also, each day an adult would be allocated to Joshua to monitor that he was kept busy, and he was to be gently reminded and encouraged to use the toilet on a regular basis.

It was agreed by both the parents and the nursery that if Joshua did a poo in his pants he was to be cleaned up and changed with no comment made. The parents would provide extra clean clothes for him. Everyone agreed that Joshua needed to be praised as much as possible to give him more self-confidence.

Joshua's mother decided she needed to give Joshua more opportunities to socialize outside of nursery, so she began inviting children from nursery once a week to play at home with Joshua.

Progress report
It was a slow process, as Joshua's confidence had taken a big knock. He had lost his playmate and, as a consequence, he was feeling very sad. He was finding it too difficult to talk about and his way of displaying his unhappiness was to hide and do a poo in his pants. Because he had always had Melissa to play with, she had always set the scene and he had just followed. He now needed to find his feet, and start making his own decisions as to what he should play and with whom. He needed help to socialize and interact with the other children. The staff did this by involving him in small group activities and turn-taking games. His parents added to this by inviting nursery friends to play at home, so he was able to practise his social skills in a different setting. Also, they ignored the negative behaviour, i.e. hiding and pooing in his pants, and praised all good behaviour to increase his self-confidence.

The outcome
In all it took about six weeks for the problem to be resolved. Joshua's parents realized there had been a breakthrough the day that Joshua announced that Melissa could have her friend from school to play and he would have his friend from nursery to play with. He was becoming more independent.

Conclusion
Joshua had always had a ready-made playmate in his older sister. When she went off to school it was almost like a bereavement

(Contd)

for him. He was terribly sad and unable to communicate this, so he had begun hiding and pooing in his pants as a way of getting everyone to notice how sad he was feeling. He had found himself in a difficult situation and had used this behaviour as a way of getting attention.

Checklist if your child is hiding and doing a poo

Here are some suggestions for you to try if you are in this situation:

▶ *Think whether there have been any changes that may have unsettled your child. Sometimes children find it hard to communicate if they are upset about what is happening around them and they may not even know why they are upset. When a child is upset about something, he may feel insecure about life and want to have more control. Doing a poo in your pants will certainly draw attention to you and put you in control.*

▶ *A positive way to move forward with your child is to ignore the poo in the pants and give him lots of extra positive praise whenever possible. You're ignoring the negative behaviour, which, let's be frank, your child is not expecting you to do, and simply praising any good behaviour so your child is more likely to stop the negative stuff. The only way to change a child's behaviour is to change yours.*

If your child is holding on to a poo

The most likely explanation is that your child is constipated so this should be the first thing you should check for. Here's a case study of a child in this situation:

Case study

Gray (two years and 11 months) was the second child in the family. He had an older brother, Maurice, aged eight years. Gray had had difficulty with pooing since he was a small baby. He had been formula fed and had been on three types of formula milk to try to resolve the problem. None of them made any difference.

The problem

Gray had suffered from constipation pretty much since birth. He had been seen by his GP and referred to the local paediatric department. There he had been examined and nothing physical had been found to be wrong. It was suggested that he was unfortunately prone to constipation, as the condition ran in the family. (Gray's mother and grandmother also suffer from constipation.) Gray had been prescribed lactulose, which had worked for a short time, and then he had begun to refuse to take it, as he did not like the taste. At this point Gray's mother was at her wits' end. If anything, the problem seemed to be getting worse and she could see no way to deal with it. Her son was extremely constipated and was holding on to his poo but would not take the treatment offered. He became very upset and said it hurt so much when he did do a poo. He was bleeding from his anus and had also begun wetting again during the day. Gray and his mum made another trip to the GP and he was diagnosed with severe constipation and an anal tear. He was now only pooing twice a week and was very grumpy and irritable for a couple of days before the poo finally came. When he did do a poo he screamed, which was, of course, very upsetting for his mother. His poos were hard and dry and often quite large.

The reason

Gray had become chronically constipated and the problem needed to be tackled from a variety of angles.

(Contd)

The solution
The solution to Gray's problem had various aspects:

1 *Gray needed to start back on the medication to soften his stool. The GP prescribed a different one in the hope that Gray would find the taste more acceptable.*
2 *Gray's mother needed to take charge of the situation and explain to Gray what had happened and why it was hurting so much when he did a poo. Also, she needed to reassure him that they could sort out the problem.*
3 *It was agreed in the short term that when Gray needed to do a poo, a nappy would be put on so that he had a sense of security.*
4 *When Gray was constipated he found it easier to poo squatting (using the pull of gravity) and was not keen to sit on the potty.*
5 *Just before he was due to do a poo, his mother was to put a good dollop of Vaseline around the outside of his anus to help the poo come out.*
6 *Whenever possible after a poo Gray would be given a warm bath to sooth and relax him.*
7 *Some minor alterations to his diet needed to be made. He had a good intake of fruit and vegetables but his favourite breakfast cereal was low in fibre. The change was to be porridge with pureed apricots. Gray also needed to increase his fluid intake.*

WEEK ONE
Gray found the new medicine more acceptable and his parents talked him through the plan with lots of reassurance that things would get better. The first couple of days were difficult. Gray had not done a poo for two days before the plan was put into action, so his parents knew that there was going to be no fast fix and that the first few poos Gray did were going to continue to be painful. On the second day he did his first poo and was very distressed. He was put into a warm bath afterwards and this did indeed help. Nothing happened the next day but on Day 4 came the next poo; standing up and having a nappy in place and using the Vaseline

did seem to aid the passing of the poo, and his mother reported that although he had been distressed, it had passed much quicker. From Day 4 onwards, Gray did a poo every day; the porridge with apricot was helping and he was taking the medication, so his constipation was eased a little, but he still had to deal with the fear and some pain.

WEEK TWO

During Week two, Gray's stools became softer and he stopped bleeding from the anal tear. He was still becoming distressed just before doing the poo and also at the beginning of the poo – his mother felt that this was partly due to the fact that it was still hurting but also that he was anticipating the pain. By the end of Week two, Gray was beginning to say that it was not hurting so much.

INTERIM PROGRESS REPORT

Gray had made excellent progress over a short span of time. All the measures that had been put in place to help him to pass the stools were working. It was reinforced to his parents that they needed to continue with all the measures, including the medication, diet and fluids and the techniques to help him pass the stools, until there was absolutely no pain and the stools were daily, soft, and easy to pass.

WEEKS THREE AND FOUR

The parents continued to follow all the advice and by the end of Week four, Gray was passing a stool once or twice each day. He was not bleeding and there was no pain. The stools were soft and easy to pass and he did not become distressed at any stage; the wetting had also stopped.

WEEK FIVE

It was now decided that Gray needed to get used to sitting down to do the poo on the potty or toilet. Gray's mother gave him the choice and he agreed to sit on the toilet. A child's toilet seat and a step was used so that his knees were bent and his feet

(Contd)

were well supported, and he was allowed to keep the nappy on while he did the poo sitting on the toilet. This continued for ten days and then Gray was finally encouraged to do a poo without the nappy.

The outcome

Gray was prone to constipation, which had got out of control and then needed a number of measures to correct it. One of the most important issues when dealing with constipation has to be keeping a close eye on the situation and maintaining measures to keep it in check. It took about two months to really sort out the problem and Gray continued on the medication for a further four months before being slowly weaned off it. However, his parents were advised that they needed to monitor Gray's bowel habits carefully, to make sure that they maintained the fibre in his diet on a daily basis and to monitor his fluid intake. They also needed to be aware that a change of environment, an illness or family stress could cause a recurrence of the problem, so they needed to remain vigilant.

Conclusion

Constipation can often be the root cause for a number of toilet training difficulties, so it is well worth ensuring that your child is not constipated before starting.

Insight

Do make sure your child is getting enough to drink, i.e. six to eight drinks – ideally milk or water – of 150 ml each spaced out during the day.

Summary

Difficulties associated with toilet training can be common. As can be seen from the variety of case studies in this chapter, there may be other factors that play a major part. Most issues can be addressed by changing the way the issue is dealt with and by putting often quite simple measures in place.

The most important message to take away from this chapter is that often a problem has been brewing for some time and that in the vast majority of cases there is no overnight miracle cure. The most effective way to deal with most toileting issues is by taking small steps and being patient. It is always necessary to take a holistic view of the situation.

10 THINGS TO REMEMBER

1 Remember that frequent wetting can be a common problem and it is important to try to work out why it is happening.

2 Restricting fluids can make the problem worse as it makes the urine concentrated and this can irritate the bladder.

3 Remember the ideal drinks for children are water and milk.

4 If your child is frequently wet, there are certain medical conditions that you need to exclude, for example, a urinary tract infection or constipation.

5 Soiling will happen in two per cent of children and it is more common in boys than in girls.

6 The most common cause of soiling is constipation.

7 Refusing to sit on the potty can be quite common. For some children the only answer is to bypass the potty phase and go straight to the toilet. Never pressurize a child to sit on the potty; it will just prove counterproductive.

8 Children often hide when doing a poo. Think about ways to make them feel comfortable about sitting on the potty to do a poo. Don't make a big fuss about it. Remember, ignoring negative behaviour and praising positive behaviour usually works.

9 When children hold on to their poo, again it is often because they are constipated and it hurts.

10 If you think your child is constipated, increase fluids and fibre. If this does not work, see your GP.

8

Night-time training

In this chapter you will learn:
- *how to tell if your child is ready for night-time training*
- *about issues that you need to consider*
- *about getting started.*

This is another exciting milestone for children and parents alike. It is another step on the path to independence and it's another opportunity for children to feel good about their achievements. Night-time training is another gradual process and there are ways to help it along, but again we need to be patient and realize that the child's body has to be ready as well.

The human body controls the amount of urine it produces at night to stop us all having to get up to use the toilet. There is a natural substance in the body called vasopressin that controls the amount of urine the kidneys produce, and at night the amount of this substance increases to slow down the flow of urine into the bladder so that it takes longer to fill. Most children's bodies develop the ability to do this at between three and five years old. All children are different; some will be dry at night a month after achieving daytime dryness, whereas others may take six months to a year to achieve night-time dryness. So, complete night-time control may not occur until four to five years of age. Approximately 90 per cent of children will be dry at night by the time they start school. That means that one in ten children in a reception class will still be wet at night. Boys tend to take longer to achieve night-time dryness than girls. If there is a family history of late night-time training this may also be a factor.

What are the signs to look for?

As with day-time readiness, there are signs for night-time readiness to look out for:

▶ *You begin to realize that your child is having the odd dry nappy in the morning.*
▶ *Your child has wet the nappy just before she wakes in the morning or as she wakes. If this is the case, the nappy will feel soaked and the urine warm.*
▶ *Your child may attempt to get up during the night to use the toilet or may call out for help.*
▶ *Your child's nappy is dry on waking from a nap – if your child is still having a nap during the day.*
▶ *Your child is reliably dry during the day.*

Insight

Night-time training will happen for most children naturally. Once their bodies start producing the hormone vasopressin, which slows down the flow of urine to the bladder, they will begin to show signs of readiness.

How to tell if your child is ready

There is absolutely no point in considering stopping putting your child in a nappy at night until she is beginning to demonstrate some or all of the above signs, especially having the odd dry nappy, or that she is weeing just before she wakes/just as she wakes, or that she is getting up during the night asking to do a wee. All of these actions show that your child's bladder is maturing and is able to hold on to a reasonable amount of urine and also that her body is beginning to produce the substance vasopressin that we talked about earlier, which controls the amount of urine the kidneys produce at night.

Again, as with daytime readiness, there are some positive steps that you can take to help your child to achieve night-time dryness:

▶ *You can encourage your child to do a wee every two hours during the day. This improves the muscle tone of the bladder and also the physical awareness that the bladder is full.*
▶ *Make sure your child is getting enough to drink and at regular intervals. See the section on Diet and drinks below.*
▶ *Check on what your child is eating in the evening. Cut out crisps or other salty foods and highly processed foods. See the section on Diet and drinks below.*

Insight

Once your child has been reliably dry during the day for three to six months, start to look for signs of night-time readiness.

Making the decision to night-train

Exactly the same principles apply to night-training as day-training. There are certain times in a child's life when it is best to avoid change. Let's revisit that list of times again.

You should avoid starting the night-time training process if:

▶ *your child is going through a negative phase*
▶ *either the child or the parent is unwell*
▶ *there is a new baby in the family*
▶ *your child is starting nursery or school*
▶ *you're undergoing a change of childcare*
▶ *you're going on holiday away from home*
▶ *you're moving house*
▶ *there has been a major family upset.*

All of these can upset you or your child – or both – and may well affect the results of your night-time toilet training efforts.

> **Insight**
>
> If you think there are some signs that your child may be ready, make sure that she is weeing regularly during the day, that there are no signs of constipation and keep an eye on what she is eating and drinking in the evening.

Equipment that may be useful

Make sure you have an extra supply of clean pyjamas or night dresses close at hand in case of accidents. Easy access to a fresh, clean sheet is also a good idea. You also need to make a decision as to whether you protect the mattress. There are two ways to do this:

First you may decide to invest in a mattress protector, which is usually a thin plastic sheet which goes over the mattress and under the bed sheet. This will protect the mattress but some children find the plastic makes them feel hot and sweaty. Also the plastic sheet may rustle when they turn in their sleep and disturb them.

A second alternative is to use an absorbent disposable change mat, which has a plastic backing. We talked about them in Chapter 3 and how they could be used to protect car seats and buggies in those early days of going out without a nappy. These are more comfortable and are less likely to make your child sweat. They can be used over the bed sheet, positioned where your child lies. If your child is prone to lots of accidents these can, however, work out as an expensive option. Also, some children move about a lot in their sleep, so it is possible for them to wriggle off the mat, resulting in a wet mattress. Specially designed disposable bed mats are now on the market – available from supermarkets and pharmacies. They are wide enough to cover the width of the bed and are held in place by 'bed wings', so these may be worth trying.

Night-clothes and nappies

Keep night-clothes simple, nothing tight and no buttons or poppers.
If your child needs a wee in the middle of the night, she is likely
to be quite drowsy so night-clothes need to be easy to pull down
and pull up. Some parents choose to use special night-time nappies
but these are often quite expensive and can give mixed messages to
your child – she may decide to use them just as she would a normal
nappy. Having said that, these night-time nappies can be useful in
the transitional period when, for a few weeks, children often wake
in the early hours of the morning to do a wee. They can be much
easier for the child to manage, as they are a bit like padded pants –
not dissimilar to the daytime training nappies. They are easier to pull
down rather than fiddling with pulling the sticky tags on a nappy.

Diet and drinks

Parents often worry that giving children lots of drinks can have an
impact on night-time dryness. But it is important that your child
does get plenty to drink during the day as this teaches your child's
bladder to hold more urine so that she will recognize the feeling of a
full bladder. Encourage your child to drink six to eight small drinks
(about 150 ml each) at regular intervals throughout the day. However,
there are certain drinks that do encourage more frequent visits to the
toilet and they are best avoided, especially in the evening. These are:

▶ *fizzy drinks*
▶ *coffee*
▶ *tea*

- *hot chocolate*
- *fruit juices, especially blackcurrant*
- *fruit squash.*

Again, as we said before, milk and water are the ideal drinks. Do let your child have a small drink in the evening before bedtime if they want one.

FOOD

Avoid salty foods in the evening as they are more likely to make your child thirsty and you may find that your child is drinking large amounts of fluids in the evening to combat this thirst. Also, it is worth avoiding processed foods with additives as these can irritate the bladder.

Getting started

So, you have decided that the time is right and your child is showing signs of readiness to go through the night without a nappy. Now is the time to start talking to your child about not wearing nappies at night. Choose a time to discuss it when your child is in a good mood. Bath time is always a good time to broach conversations like this, as your child is relaxed and usually happy. Put it in a positive light, talk about how grown up she will be and that mummy and daddy or older siblings don't wear nappies in bed. She may show signs of being worried if she has an accident; tell her about your plans to protect the mattress and that there will be clean night clothes and a sheet if this happens. Also, make a big fuss of reassuring her that if she does have an accident you will not be cross with her.

Before starting, let's look at that checklist again:

- *Your child is reliably dry during the day, wees every two hours or so and does not have more than the occasional accident.*
- *Your child is having a good fluid intake.*
- *You have checked her diet and fluid intake in the evening and overhauled it if it has been required.*

- *You are getting the odd dry nappy in the morning or your child is beginning to wake you up during the night for her to use the toilet.*
- *When you change your child's nappy in the morning, it is clear that she has recently done a wee.*
- *Life is calm and no changes or family upsets are on the horizon.*

The golden rule is SEVEN NIGHTS WITH A DRY NAPPY before you take the bull by the horns and stop using nappies. You need to make a decision with your child as to how you are going to tackle the night-times if she needs to get up and do a wee and you need to have a clear procedure in place. The next section will give you some ideas as to how to do this.

Night-time waking

Some children will go through a transition period of waking at night to do a wee. It is very tempting in the middle of the night when you are tired and you have to get up for work, or you have already been up with a younger child, to say 'Oh, just do it in your nappy'. However tempting this is, it will not help your child to achieve night-time dryness. This waking up is only a phase and it will pass.

So what is the best way to deal with night-time waking? You and your child have a choice of having a potty in the bedroom or of her getting up and going to the bathroom to use the toilet.

Let's look at the two options:

1 HAVING A POTTY IN THE BEDROOM

If you are going to use a potty in the bedroom for night-time waking you need to consider the following:

- *The potty should always be left in the same place.*
- *You will need to remind your child every evening when you say good night that the potty is there.*

- Decide if you are going to have a night light, a dimmer switch or a torch so that your child can see what she is doing. If you decide on a torch, again make sure that she knows where it is and that the batteries are not flat.
- Your child will need some toilet roll or wipes so that she can clean herself after her wee.
- Wipes can also be used to clean her hands after a wee.

Parent's comment

We had a potty in the bedroom at night and used a night light. I was not keen on the idea of Fin wandering around the house and I was really concerned about the stairs. It worked fine, although we did have the odd time when the potty got knocked over.

2 USING THE TOILET FOR NIGHT-TIME WAKING

If your child is going to go to the toilet you will need to consider the following:

- Can she open the bedroom and bathroom doors easily?
- If you are going to use a torch to help her find her way, make sure she knows where the torch is and that the batteries are not flat.
- Think about the sort of access that you have to the toilet – does your child have to go up or down stairs and, if so, is she confident doing so?
- You may decide to leave a light on in the hallway instead.
- Make a decision if the toilet is going to be flushed after use – if there are other sleeping children the flushing of the toilet may wake them up.

An all-important decision to be made is: do you want to help your child or does she need your help during the night? If you decide that you want her to tell you if she needs a wee during the night so that you can help her, then you will need to make it clear to her how she does this. Does she call for help or does she come into your bedroom and wake you up? If you decide that your child can manage on her own during the night, it makes sense to use the night-time training nappies. Even the most dexterous of children would struggle with putting a nappy back on.

Once you have made the decisions as to how you are going to deal with night-time waking to do a wee, discuss it with your child. When she's going to bed for the first few nights remind her what the procedure is until she is really confident about what she is doing.

Insight

Make sure you have taken the time to talk through with your child what is going to happen. Getting up to do a wee in the night is very different to doing one during the day. She needs to be clear about the plan – does she wake you? Are you going to use a night light? There is a lot to think about.

To lift or not to lift

Some parents lift their children in the evening before they themselves go to bed. By this we mean the parent lifts the child out of bed while she is still asleep and puts her on the toilet in an attempt to get her to empty her bladder so that she is less likely to wet during the night. Some parents swear by this method whereas other parents find it not so useful. If you are going to use this method the key to it is that your child should be sufficiently awake when you take her to the toilet to realize that she is doing a wee. This is because there is then more chance that she will empty her bladder. If your child is sound asleep then she is unlikely to do a wee or if she does, it is likely to be a small one and the bladder will not empty, so will have little effect on night-time dryness. Of course, the downside is that you may need to wake your child up to the extent that she finds it difficult to settle back to sleep.

Parent's comments

I always lifted my children for the first few weeks and have never had any wet beds.

Jo – mother of three boys

It worked for my daughter but I found it impossible to get it right with my son. Either he was so sound asleep that he did not do a wee or the couple of times when we managed to wake him up enough to get a wee out of him, he would not go back to sleep. So we gave up on that idea with him.

Trish – mother of Clara and Oscar

Making progress

Let's look at how night-time training might go:

WEEK ONE

Night 1

Everything is in place; your child is regularly going to the toilet during the day and is having only occasional, or no, accidents during the day. You have had the odd dry nappy or maybe your child has woken to do a wee in the night. You have decided if you are going to lift your child before you go to bed. A procedure has been worked out and agreed for if your child wakes up during the night. The type of fluids that your child drinks during the evening has been reviewed and changes made if necessary.

Don't forget that at this stage your child will still have a nappy on at night. You do not stop using a nappy until you have had *seven dry nights.*

Have a chat with your child that evening before bed about staying dry at night. Remind her that she can get up to do a wee in the potty or toilet if she needs to during the night. Whichever you have decided, whether it is a potty in her bedroom or if she is going to get up and use the toilet, go through the procedure with her of what she does if she needs a wee during the night.

DURING THE NIGHT
If she wakes to do a wee, make sure you give her lots of praise.

If she wakes to say she has done a wee in her nappy then that is still progress because the sensation of weeing has woken her up. Praise her for this too and tell her that soon she will wake up before she wees and will be able to use the potty or toilet.

IN THE MORNING
When you get up go straight away and check if her nappy is dry. If it is dry encourage her to do a wee as soon as possible. If the nappy

is wet, check and see if it is warm, as she may have just done it. If it is still warm then gently remind her that she can do this wee in the potty or toilet.

Nights 2–7

Keep a note of which nights are dry. Don't forget to monitor what she is drinking in the evenings. You do not have to restrict her fluid intake but just make sure she is not having any of the drinks listed that will make her wee more, and that she is being offered milk or water only.

If you are finding that she is still wet in the morning but it does appear warm and if you have not been lifting her before you go to bed, then it may well be worth trying this. The whole night may be just a little too long for her just yet.

Evaluating progress

By the end of the week (seven nights) you will be getting a picture as to whether your child is reaching night-time dryness. Ask yourself the following questions:

1 *Have there been any dry nights?*
2 *Does she wake in the night needing to do a wee?*
3 *Has she woken because she has done a wee in her nappy?*
4 *In the morning when you go to her room has she recently done a wee in her nappy?*

If you have answered yes to any of the above, night-time readiness is coming.

Obviously, if she is occasionally having dry nappies, she is almost there. Once there are seven consecutive nights of dry nappies, you can stop using the nappies but think about a mattress protector. Remember, it is not uncommon for some children to go through a period of waking in the early hours of the morning to do a wee. This is a transitional period and it will stop after a matter of weeks as the bladder learns to hold on to more urine during the night. Go with it and encourage her to get up and do a wee if she needs to. The urge to get up during the night will stop.

If your child is waking because she has done a wee in the nappy or if she does one just on waking in the morning, try lifting her – it may be that the night is just a little too long. Don't forget that if you are lifting her, she needs to be aware that she is doing a wee so that she empties her bladder as much as possible.

If, at the end of the week, you find that your child is not showing any signs of progress, don't worry! One in ten children will start school and still need a nappy at night, so it's far from uncommon. In most cases it will sort itself out during the reception year at school. If it does not and your child is over the age of five years, read the section in Chapter 9 on nocturnal enuresis.

Insight

Remember that children can have relapses at night just the same as during the day – and for the same reasons. The key is to find the reason for the relapses and resolve the issue rather than simply putting them back in nappies.

Case study: ready for night-training

Malachi had a younger sibling, a sister called Mariah who was 12 months old.

The problem
Malachi (four years and two months) was showing signs of readiness for night-time training but just as his parents were going to start, he would have a couple of random nights of soaking wet nappies. There did not appear to be a pattern and his parents were not sure whether to start or not.

The reason
Malachi was drinking orange squash in the evenings, which was making him pass more urine than he needed to.

(Contd)

The solution

We needed to identify if Malachi was ready. He was having two to three dry nights each week. On the mornings when he was wet it was clear that he had recently wet the nappy, as it was very full and warm to touch. He was not waking during the night to do a wee but he clearly appeared to be moving towards night-time readiness. His parents were keen to have a go at training him at night.

WEEK ONE

▶ *Malachi was encouraged during the day to have a wee every two hours or so. He was not prone to accidents.*

▶ *Malachi often drank orange squash in the evening; this was stopped and water or milk was offered.*

▶ *It was agreed that his parents would lift him before they went to bed at 11 p.m. (Malachi's bedtime was 8 p.m.). When he was lifted he needed to be awake long enough to realize that he was doing a wee. This action was taken because Malachi sometimes woke in the morning having just done a wee in his nappy.*

INTERIM PROGRESS REPORT

The week went well and Malachi responded to being lifted before his parents went to bed. On Days 3, 4, 5, 6 and 7 he had a dry nappy in the morning.

WEEK TWO

▶ *It was agreed that Malachi needed to have seven dry nights before his nappy was taken off.*

▶ *His parents were to continue lifting him each evening.*

▶ *They were to also continue to encourage him to go to the toilet every two hours during the day.*

▶ *Milk and water were the only drinks that he was to continue to have in the evenings.*

INTERIM PROGRESS REPORT

Malachi managed six dry nights and was wet on the seventh. Although his parents were disappointed they agreed to start counting again.

By the end of the third week, Malachi had seven consecutive dry nights.

His parents were then advised to stop the nappies at night but to continue to lift him for a further two weeks, which they did. They were also advised to protect the mattress.

WEEK SIX
▶ *Malachi's parents had a discussion with him about stopping the lifting at night-time.*
▶ *It was agreed that if he woke to do a wee in the night, he was to call his parents and one of them would take him to the toilet.*

The outcome
Week six went well and aside from one accident on the third night Malachi woke each night at approximately 3 a.m. for a wee. This continued for approximately two weeks, after which he was able to sleep through until 7–7.30 a.m. without waking to do a wee or having an accident.

Conclusion
The types of drinks that children have really can impact on toilet training and simply stopping certain types of drinks can result in success.

Insight
Again, you may find keeping a diary helpful. It can show the pattern of what is happening and help you to make changes that will enable success.

Frequently asked questions

Q1: *I am thinking about night training my three-and-a-half-year-old and a friend has advised me to restrict his drinks in the*

evening and not let him drink anything after 5 p.m. Is that
what I should do?

It is a bit of a myth that restricting a child's fluids in the evening will result in a dry nappy overnight. By restricting fluids you will make your child's urine concentrated and this in turn may well irritate the bladder and make your child wee more frequently. Be selective as to what your child drinks in the evening – the best choices are water or milk, but it is important that your child is well hydrated so do let him have a small drink before bedtime if he wants it.

Q2: *Is it worth protecting the mattress when my child stops*
wearing nappies at night-time? She never had any accidents
when we stopped the day-time nappies.

You are lucky. It is very unusual for a child never to have an accident so it is worth protecting the mattress. To stay dry all night, every night, is a huge achievement and it is not uncommon for children to wet when they are unwell. So for your daughter's comfort and to make life easier for yourself, it is worth thinking about a mattress protector.

Summary

Night-time training is, in a sense, no different to day-time training. The body has to be ready and again it is a physical developmental stage, over which we have no control. However, as with daytime training there are areas that can be fine-tuned. Making sure your child understands what is expected of her and that clear procedures are in place for night-time waking are two things parents can do to help. They can also help their child to develop the self-help skills of managing night-clothes, and an overhaul of the types of fluid that their child is drinking in the evening can, if needed, be carried out.

If your child is over five years of age and has, as yet, not acquired night-time dryness then read the section in Chapter 9 on nocturnal enuresis for further advice.

10 THINGS TO REMEMBER

1   Remember the signs to look out for – the occasional dry nappy in the morning, a 'just wet' nappy on waking (it will feel warm), waking in the night and asking to use the toilet, waking from a daytime nap with a dry nappy and being reliably dry during the day.

2   Your child needs to be showing some or all of the above signs before she is ready to do without nappies at night-time.

3   Do make sure that your child is getting enough to drink and that in the evening she is not being given any drinks that may irritate the bladder.

4   Avoid salty foods in the evening as they are more likely to make your child thirsty.

5   It is important that you choose the right time to night train, with no major changes or problems happening – or about to happen – in your child's life.

6   Think in advance about the equipment you will need. Protecting the mattress is important. Keep night clothing simple and have changes available as well as clean sheets/bedding.

7   When you decide to start make sure you have talked to your child about what is going to happen.

8   Decide how you are going to manage night-time waking. Are you going to leave a potty in the room, for example, or will your child get up and go to the toilet? Think about having a night light.

9   Remember the golden rule – SEVEN DRY NIGHTS IN A ROW – before you stop using nappies.

10 Decide if you want to lift or not lift your child before you go to bed.

9

The school-age child

In this chapter you will learn:
- *about independence skills*
- *how and why a child may relapse*
- *about nocturnal enuresis.*

Independence skills

Starting school opens up a whole new world for children and they face many challenges. This can be both exciting and scary for child and parent alike. Making sure that your child is well prepared for those changes can be nothing but beneficial.

> **Insight**
> Make sure your child is independent in toileting before he starts school. School is a brand new experience and makes lots of demands. A child who is confident in toileting has one less thing to worry about.

Many parents feel that what children need most of all to be able to do well when they are first at school is to know the alphabet and be able to count. Of course, these things are important, but in fact what is far more useful for a child is for him to be independent in his toileting, to be able to feed himself and to be able to sit for a short time and concentrate.

When we talk about being independent in toileting it means:

- *Being reliably dry and clean during the day.*
- *Knowing when he needs the toilet and responding to that need straight away.*
- *Being able to communicate effectively that he needs to go to the toilet.*
- *When he reaches the toilet, being able to pull down his clothes and pull them up again.*
- *Being able to clean himself after a wee or a poo.*
- *Knowing how to wash his hands thoroughly and always doing it.*

You can help your child to achieve all these skills before he starts school. It will be a great help to him to be confident in toileting and will also be a boost to his self-esteem that he can just get on with it. Another advantage is that it will be hugely helpful to the class teacher. Can you imagine, there are going to be probably 30 or so four- to five-year-olds in your child's class? There will be one teacher and one nursery nurse/teaching assistant. If all 30 children need help every time they go to the toilet then not much else would get done!

....

Insight

True independence is not just about being clean and dry. It is all the other skills as well – the ability to get dressed and undressed, to wipe yourself and to wash hands properly.

....

So, let's go back and look in a bit more detail at the skills needed to be independent at toileting.

- **Being reliably dry and clean** – *most children reach this stage by the time they go to school, but it is not uncommon for them to have the odd accident. Making sure they go to the toilet on a regular basis will help to increase reliability. So, always, first thing on waking, remind them to do a wee and check if they need another wee before leaving for school. Remind them to* do a wee at breaks and lunchtime. Get them into the habit of going for a wee every two hours or so. You will find that your child's day is naturally broken up into periods of roughly two hours with playtimes at school, lunch breaks, home time, tea time, bed time and so on, so this should be quite easy to organize. Also, make sure you leave enough time in the morning if that is when they tend to have a poo.

▶ **Knowing when they need the toilet and responding to that need straight away** – *many children delay doing a wee even after they become aware of the need because they are too busy playing. Encourage them when they show signs – for example, when they begin jiggling about – to go to the toilet without delay. Talk to them about the importance of doing it straight away if they feel they need a wee or a poo.*

▶ **Being able to communicate effectively that they need to go to the toilet** – *many children are often shy in a new environment and many an accident has happened because they have not had the confidence to ask to go for a wee. School is not like nursery where a child can just wander from one play area to another, and also go off and do a wee whenever he feels like it. School, even in the reception class, is a much more structured environment and there will be times when your child is expected to sit on the carpet or at a table to undertake an activity. He will not be able to wander in and out of the classrooms. So, your child needs to be able to communicate effectively in all circumstances if he needs to go to the toilet.*

A little role-play session before starting school can help immensely with this. So, pretend you are the child and your child is the teacher. Show him how you put your hand up to get attention and ask to go to the toilet. Then swap roles and let him have a go at asking. Practise this a few times so that your child feels confident.

▶ **Being able to dress and undress themselves** – *if your child has a uniform, make sure the trousers or skirt are big enough and,* *for girls who wear tights, that they are easy to pull up. Again practise at home. If there is no uniform be selective about what your child wears in the first few weeks of term. Again, easy-to-deal-with clothes are essential. No difficult buttons, poppers, zips or dungarees.*

▶ **Being able to clean themselves after a poo** – *this is quite a difficult task. Children often find this hard, as their arms are just not long enough. The staff in school are usually unable to help with this, so it really is important that your child has mastered this skill before starting school. Again, lots of practice and help on your part will help. Don't be cross if, in the first few weeks, you find poo-stained pants or knickers – they just need more practice.*

▶ **Knowing how to wash their hands** – *we have spoken before about the importance of hand-washing (in Chapter 6). Do make sure your child is competent at this skill – it really does prevent infection.*

Relapse

It is fairly common for children to have the odd accident, whether it is a wee or a poo, during the first few weeks at school. It is nothing to worry about. The teachers and support staff will deal with the situation and reassure your child.

Relapses of toileting can happen for a whole host of reasons including:

▶ *Unfamiliar environment – not knowing where the toilet is.*
▶ *Getting used to the routine – so not being able to wander off whenever they need to go to the toilet.*
▶ *Not feeling confident enough to ask to go to the toilet.*
▶ *Being excited by what they are doing and forgetting to go.*
▶ *Feeling tired – this is very common.*
▶ *Urinary tract infections can cause wetting.*

Parents' comments

'Mohamed found the first couple of weeks at school quite difficult as he is very shy. He found it hard to ask if he needed to go to the toilet, as he does not speak much English. But now he knows where to go, so we have not had any more accidents.'

'Arben just got so tired. It was not uncommon for him to fall asleep at the end of the day when the teacher was reading the class a story. He tended to have an accident towards the end of the week. Now that he has been at school for a term it is getting much better, but we still get the odd bag of wet clothes at the end of the day.'

'I found Siobhan got a bit constipated when she first started school. She said she did not like doing a poo in the school toilets, as they were so busy with children in and out all the time. We got into the habit of getting up a bit earlier and making sure she had time to sit on the toilet at home to do a poo if she needed. It seemed to help at the time.'

Most relapses are short-lived and they sort themselves out. However, if you feel concerned, or if your child appears to be having more than the odd accident, make an appointment with the class teacher and have a chat about it. He or she will be able to share their expertise and experience in this area and together you will be able to put together a plan to deal with the issue.

For some children, a relapse may be due to a number of factors that have happened around the same time, and the relapse may be a sign that the child has simply become overwhelmed with all that is going on in his life at that moment in time.

It is not uncommon for children to relapse when they start school. Don't get cross with your child – he is not doing it on purpose. A chat with the child's teacher may help you to resolve the issue.

Case study: soiling at school

Craig (five years and two months) was an only child. His parents were going through a difficult divorce and Craig had moved, with his mother, to be closer to his maternal grandparents. He had recently started school and was the only child in the reception class who had not attended the nursery there.

The problem
Craig was soiling at school two or three times a week. He appeared unconcerned about this and his mother had tried a number of strategies in an attempt to deal with it, which ranged from ignoring the soiling to getting very cross with Craig. Nothing appeared to work.

The previous few months had been very unsettled for Craig. Craig and his mother had moved to be close to his maternal grandparents who had offered to help with childcare. Craig's mother worked full-time and had to leave the house at 7.15 a.m., when she would drop Craig at her parents' house. She did not get back to collect Craig until 7 p.m. at night. Her parents did the taking to and fetching from school.

Craig's father had visiting access, but often let Craig down at the last minute. He was missing his dad enormously and his behaviour would often become quite difficult after he had spent time with his father.

Craig's teacher reported that Craig was often inattentive in class and was finding it difficult to make friends. As all the children had

(Contd)

already been at nursery together, friendship groups had been formed and Craig was finding it a challenge to break into a friendship group.

Craig's mother was exhausted. She was working full-time and her travel time to and from work had increased because their new home was further away from where she was working. She felt unsupported by Craig's father and felt she could not rely on him. Her parents had been very willing to help but she was concerned that it might be too much for them. Her parents were the ones having to deal with collecting him from school to be told that he had soiled again.

The reason
It was felt that Craig was soiling because he felt that he had lost control over his world. His dad was not around as he used to be. Sometimes when he was due to see him, his father did not turn up, plus there was a new house and a new school to deal with. He was also missing his old friends at the nursery that he had attended since he was two. Soiling was his way of having some control over what was happening.

The solution
Craig's mother was advised by the school that Craig should be seen by his GP to exclude a physical reason for the soiling, for example, constipation. This she did and the GP felt sure that Craig was not constipated and that his soiling was a result of many months of change and turmoil.

There were a number of areas that needed to be addressed and they were broken down as follows:

THE SOILING
It was agreed by everyone that the soiling was to be ignored when it happened and that Craig's clothing would be changed without comment.

BEHAVIOUR
Craig's parents, his grandparents and the class teacher were all asked to praise Craig at any sign of positive behaviour and to

ignore, where possible, any negative behaviour. A star chart was introduced both at school and at home to reward good behaviour. If Craig received enough stars during the week he was allowed a treat at the weekend that he had a choice in. Craig was given special jobs to do in class and around the school. The aim of these actions was to increase Craig's sense of control over what was happening, so, if he behaved well, he could control the number of stars and had some control in the choice of treat that he was given.

FRIENDSHIPS

In class he was encouraged to work in small groups to develop friendships. Some of the group work was done as turn-taking games to improve his concentration. When he was asked to do a special job in class or around the school, he was allowed to choose a friend to help him.

His mother agreed that at weekends she would arrange play dates for Craig so that he had the opportunity to develop some friendships on a one-to-one basis. The aim of these actions was to give Craig lots of opportunity to develop friendships.

CRAIG'S PARENTS

The need for the parents to sort out their differences had been highlighted and they agreed to counselling. Craig's father took on board that letting Craig down was compounding his son's problems and that he needed to act in a more responsible manner. This was crucial to the plan working, as Craig clearly felt let down by his father's actions.

GRANDPARENTS

Craig's grandparents were doing a terrific job of supporting their daughter but they were finding it tiring. Craig's mother agreed with her workplace to cut down her hours slightly so that she finished early on a Friday and was able to collect Craig from school. This gave the grandparents some respite and also allowed Craig's mother the opportunity to communicate with Craig's teacher effectively at the end of every week.

(Contd)

The outcome

This little boy's life had been turned upside down by the break-up of his parents' marriage. Not only did he have to cope with his father not being around for him and at times letting him down, he also had to cope with a house move and a new school where, as the newcomer, he felt socially isolated. His self-esteem and confidence had taken an enormous knock – soiling was his cry for help.

It took time for the plan to have an effect. His parents, grandparents and the school all worked very hard at increasing his self-esteem and confidence. Slowly he began to make friends and his concentration in class improved. The relationship between his parents became more amicable when it became apparent how damaging it had been for Craig.

The soiling continued for some months but as things settled and Craig began to feel secure and more in control of what was happening in his life, the soiling became less and less frequent until it eventually stopped.

Conclusion

Most soiling is due to constipation, but occasionally it can be due to emotional issues. When this is the case, it is important to identify what the trigger has been and to seek professional help to resolve the situation.

Insight

In every reception class, one in ten children will not be dry at night. So, in a typical class of 30, there will be at least three children who still wet at night-time.

What is nocturnal enuresis?

Nocturnal enuresis is bedwetting that occurs during sleep in a child aged five years and over. Primary nocturnal enuresis is when a child has never been consistently dry at night and secondary nocturnal enuresis is when a child has been dry for at least six months and has then started to have bedwetting episodes.

It is estimated that about 500,000 children in the UK suffer from persistent nocturnal enuresis.

Incidence of nocturnal enuresis

Children aged 5	1 in 6 children
Children aged 7	1 in 7 children
Children aged 9	1 in 11 children
Teenagers	1 in 50 teenagers

Source: Department of Health 2000

For young children, bedwetting can be very humiliating and upsetting. It may also, understandably, lead to a huge amount of stress and frustration in the family, not to mention trying to cope with frequent bed changing, extra washing and dealing with an upset child in the middle of the night.

A child may fear that he will be discovered by friends and miss out on sleepovers and school trips. Bedwetting needs to be quickly resolved. If it is allowed to continue, children may lose confidence and develop a low self-esteem.

What are the causes of bedwetting?

Primary nocturnal enuresis (when a child has never been consistently dry) is usually the result of one of the following:

Unable to wake from sleep – some children simply do not wake during the night when their bladder is full:

▶ *Inability to wake to a full bladder sensation.*
▶ *Sleeping through wetting.*

Overactive (irritable) bladder or a small bladder capacity – children with this condition often present with these symptoms:

- ▶ *Sense of urgency (dashing to the toilet).*
- ▶ *Needing to wee more than seven times per day.*
- ▶ *Small amount of urine at each wee.*
- ▶ *Lots of wetting episodes at night.*
- ▶ *Wet patches of different sizes.*
- ▶ *Wakes after wetting the bed.*

Low vasopressin hormone at night – this is the hormone that is produced by the kidneys to slow down the amount of urine made during the night:

- ▶ *Wets soon after falling asleep.*
- ▶ *Large wet patches.*
- ▶ *Dry nights only if the child wakes up at night to go to the toilet.*

Primary nocturnal enuresis can often be genetic, i.e. it runs in the family. If one parent suffered with it, then there is a 40 per cent risk of a child being affected; if both parents were sufferers, then there is a 75 per cent risk.

Secondary nocturnal enuresis (where a child has been dry at night for six months or more and then relapses) may be caused by a stressful event or by a urinary tract problem.

Whether your child is suffering from primary or secondary nocturnal enuresis your GP is the best person to help you to find out what is causing the problem, and he or she will give appropriate support, advice and treatment.

The really good news is that nocturnal enuresis can now be effectively treated. Once the reason for a child's bedwetting is understood, the most appropriate and effective treatment can be employed.

School Nurse-Led Enuresis Clinic

Some Primary Care Trusts run School Nurse-led Enuresis Clinics. These clinics are run by qualified nurses who have a special interest in enuresis. You can refer yourself and your child directly to the clinic; this is called a self-referral. Alternatively, your GP or school can also refer your child for you; the clinic will see children aged 5–19 years.

The advantage of this clinic is that a professional, who has experience in this particular field, will support you and your child. The clinic will be held at a local health centre and your referral will be in the strictest confidence.

On your first visit with your child, a detailed history will be taken and, in the first instance, conservative treatment to develop bladder control will be recommended. This could include:

▶ *increase daytime drinking*
▶ *establish a regular toileting routine – going to the toilet each break time at school and every two to three hours at home*
▶ *a review of drinks in the evenings*
▶ *no nappies at night.*

Your child will receive a diary in which to record his dry nights (the whole emphasis is on the positive, so that is why wet nights are not recorded). He may also be given an incentive chart with stickers. Often, improving bladder control and increasing a child's fluid intake is all that is needed. A follow-up appointment will be made to discuss the dry-nights diary and then to plan further treatment as required.

Treatment for primary nocturnal enuresis

ENURESIS ALARM

An enuresis alarm is a battery-operated device that is often used to treat children with bedwetting problems. The alarm goes off as

soon as the child starts to wet the bed. The alarm wakes
the child up and he begins to learn to recognize the sensation of
a full bladder. There are two types of alarm available: bed mat,
where a detector mat is placed under the bed sheet; or a body-worn
alarm. Both types of alarm have a noise box that sounds as soon
as the child begins to wet. Gradually the child learns to wake up
and hold on to the sensation of a full bladder without the alarm.
The most appropriate age to start using an alarm is around seven
years of age as the alarm has been found to be most effective and
successful in this age group. However, alarms have been used
successfully for children aged five upwards with parental support.
You will need to be prepared for some disrupted nights' sleep
until the routine is established and the alarm begins to result
in dry nights. About two thirds of children achieve success
whilst using the alarm. Success is defined as being dry for 14
consecutive nights. The factors that will indicate a high possibility
of success are:

- *no behavioural issues*
- *normal functional bladder capacity*
- *no daytime wetting*
- *wets later at night.*

Generally a child improves and then becomes dry within six to
eight weeks, but it may take longer. You will see signs of progress
such as the child waking to the alarm and he will have smaller wet
patches than previously.

DESMOPRESSIN

Desmopressin is a medicine that can be recommended by the
School Nurse-Led Enuresis Clinic and prescribed by your GP.
It is similar to vasopressin, a hormone that is naturally released
during sleep. It acts to reduce the volume of urine produced at
night to a level more 'manageable' for the child. The medicine
works for about eight hours. Seven out of ten children show
rapid improvement whilst taking the medicine.

Top tips to overcome bed-wetting

▶ *Make sure your child drinks plenty of fluids – six to eight small drinks during the day. This will teach your child's bladder to hold more urine so that he will begin to recognize the feeling of a full bladder.*

▶ *Make sure your child avoids fizzy drinks, coffee, tea, hot chocolate and blackcurrant, as these will make him go to the toilet more often. Give your child a small drink in the evening before bedtime.*

▶ *Make sure your child has a wee just before bedtime.*

▶ *Make going to the toilet easy, using a torch or leaving a light on.*

▶ *Your child should not be wearing nappies or pull-ups.*

▶ *Protect the mattress, duvet and pillows.*

▶ *Have fresh nightclothes and bed linen on hand.*

▶ *If your child has wet the bed, let him have a bath or shower in the morning before school.*

▶ *Avoid constipation.*

Insight

If you have tried all the top tips for night-time dryness and your child is over five years old and still wetting at night, do look into a referral to the local enuresis clinic.

Campaigns in schools

The charity ERIC (Education and Resources for Improving Childhood Continence) is working hard to promote two campaigns in schools. The 'Water is Cool in School' campaign encourages schools to allow pupils to each have a bottle of water in class. The aims of the campaign are as follows:

▶ *To increase public awareness of the health benefits to children of drinking good levels of water regularly during the school day.*

- ▶ *To improve the quality of provision and access to fresh drinking water in primary and secondary schools.*
- ▶ *To obtain comprehensive legislation on drinking facilities in schools.*

If the school your child attends is not part of this campaign, why not tell them about it and they can contact ERIC for an information pack.

The other campaign is 'Bog Standard', which is a campaign to promote better toilets for pupils. The aims of the campaign are as follows:

- ▶ *To increase awareness of the health benefits of better toilets for pupils.*
- ▶ *To encourage schools to improve the condition of pupils' toilets and to allow pupils to use them when they need to.*
- ▶ *To get laws that will make pupils' toilets nicer to use.*

Details of the ERIC website and other sources of help are given in the 'Taking it further' section at the back of this book.

Case study: wet at night

Adam (eight years) was the middle child of three with an older sister, Becky, aged 11 years, and a brother, Toby, aged two years.

The problem
Adam had never been consistently dry at night. He had maybe two or three nights a week when he was dry – more noticeably at the weekend. The other nights he would be wet. He appeared to sleep through the wetting. It was beginning to bother him and he had recently missed out on a sleepover birthday party as he did not want his friends to know he wet the bed.

The reason
Adam's parents had always been quite relaxed about his bedwetting. They did not think there was a physical reason, just that Adam was a very sound sleeper. He did have nights when

he was dry but there was no consistency to them, although, on reflection, he was more likely to be dry on a weekend night. It was only when he became upset about missing the birthday sleepover that his parents decided that maybe it was time to tackle the issue.

Adam was a very physically active child who loved all sports. He did many after-school activities which all revolved around sport – football, gym, and multi-sports. He would rush around, getting very hot and drinking copious amounts of juice and blackcurrant drinks.

Adam tended to settle quite early for an eight-year-old and was often sound asleep by 7.30 p.m.

The solution
Three simple measures were put in place.
1 *Adam was only allowed to drink water after his sporting activities. The juice and blackcurrant drinks were stopped.*
2 *Just before going to bed, Adam was encouraged to go to the toilet.*
3 *Before his parents went to bed, about 11 p.m., one of them would lift Adam and make sure he was awake enough to do a wee on the toilet.*

Progress and outcome
It helped greatly that Adam also wanted the problem resolved. He had been very upset about missing the sleepover party and was determined to tackle the night-time wetting. He accepted that he needed to change his choice of drinks after sports. It took a few attempts at night to wake him enough to do a wee, but once he was consistently weeing when his parents lifted him, he was able to stay dry for the rest of the night. It took a month to achieve seven dry nights in a row. Then his parents stopped lifting him. For a short period of time he woke at about 2 a.m. for a wee but after a couple of weeks that stopped and he was able to sleep through. However, his parents did notice that if ever Adam had blackcurrant or a fizzy drink in the evening he was much more likely to need to get up during the night for a wee.

(Contd)

Conclusion

For Adam the realization that because of his bed-wetting he was missing out on fun things was the turning point. An important factor with night-time training is that a child really wants to be dry.

Frequently asked questions

Q1: *My son is almost five and is due to start school in the next few months. He still wets the bed at night. Is this normal and should I do anything about it?*

Approximately one in ten children aged five will wet the bed at night, so in a reception class of 30, the likelihood is that there will be at least three children who are not dry at night. For most children it just takes time for them to acquire night-time dryness, but there are things that you can do to help your child on his way. Make sure he is getting plenty of fluids during the day – at least six to eight small drinks spread out at regular intervals throughout the day. In the evenings, restrict his choice of fluids to milk or water only. Fizzy drinks and fruit juices, or any drink that contains caffeine, will make your child want to wee more frequently. If he wants a drink in the evening before bed, let him have it. Make sure he goes to the toilet just before he is due to go to bed and you can try lifting him before you go to bed to see if that helps. If, by the time he turns five, and after trying all these suggestions, he is not showing any signs of night-time dryness, you may decide to have a chat with the school nurse or your GP for further advice.

Q2: *My seven-year-old daughter has never been dry at night and it is now beginning to upset her as she would like to have a friend to sleep over but she is embarrassed as she still wears nappies. What can I do to help?*

First of all check what she is eating and drinking. Is she constipated? Make sure she is having enough fibre in her diet. If possible cut out all fizzy drinks, fruit juice and any drinks that contain caffeine, as these will all make her wee more frequently. Get her to do a wee before going to bed and stop the nappies. Protect the mattress and keep a diary of the wetting at night. So, note if there are any dry nights, when she has a wet night, what time of night it happens and whether it is a large amount or lots of little wees.

If the wetting does not improve with the simple measures that you have put in place, see your GP with the diary and ask for a referral to an enuresis clinic.

Q3: *My son is in reception class at school and will not use the school toilet to do a poo. He is becoming constipated and I am not sure what to do about it. Any ideas?*

Try to find out what is worrying him about using the school toilet. It may be that he feels rushed or that the toilets are very busy. Go in and talk to the class teacher – other children may also be having the same difficulties. Maybe the school could arrange for an adult to be near the toilets during break time so that if a child needs privacy this can be arranged. Does your child feel confident in asking to go to the toilet? Maybe a little role-play and practising how to ask may help. If constipation is a problem, sort it out; make sure your child is having enough fluids and plenty of fibre. One idea is to get up a little earlier in the morning and give your child the opportunity to sit on the toilet about 15–20 minutes after breakfast to see if he needs to do a poo. If you can get him into the routine of doing a poo in the morning before leaving for school this may well solve all your problems.

Summary

In this chapter we have concentrated on the problem of bedwetting and how to deal with it. Bedwetting in a child over five years of age is a fairly common problem but there is help available to support parents dealing with this situation.

10 THINGS TO REMEMBER

1 Toilet training is not just about a child being able to do a wee or poo in the potty. It is also about him being able to pull his clothes up and down, to wipe himself and to wash his hands properly.

2 Being independent in toileting when starting school is a big plus for your child.

3 It is not uncommon for children to have a relapse with toileting when they first start school.

4 If your child does have a relapse, go and have a chat with the class teacher. She will be very experienced with this issue and together you can look at ways to help your child.

5 Nocturnal enuresis is when a child over five years of age wets during sleep.

6 One in six children aged five will still wet at night-time so it is not uncommon.

7 There are three main causes of night-time wetting – where a child is unable to wake from sleep, where a child has an irritable or small bladder or has low levels of the hormone vasopressin at night.

8 If your child is suffering from nocturnal enuresis then do seek help. Some areas have school nurse-led clinics or your GP will be able to help.

9 Many schools now take part in the 'Water is Cool in School' campaign, which helps to promote the importance of children drinking water.

10 The other school campaign in this area is 'Bog Standard', which aims to improve the standard of school toilets.

10

Children with special needs

In this chapter you will learn:
- *about toileting techniques for your child with a physical disability*
- *about toileting techniques for your child with a learning disability*
- *about resources that you may find useful.*

All children with special needs, whether a physical disability or a learning disability, have the right to reach their own personal potential in all areas of their development. The challenge in the area of toilet training for a parent of a child with special needs is to work out the best approach, at the most helpful time, for their child in order to achieve bladder and bowel control.

For children with special needs all the same principles apply in relation to toilet training; whatever your child's abilities and disabilities, she needs to have the skills in place to successfully toilet train. It may mean, however, that your child will train later, after she has acquired those skills. It may also mean that you as a parent will need to take a much more organized approach to toilet training in that the toileting routine needs to be very firmly established, and your child will need support for a bit longer before she is able to initiate the routine herself. In this chapter we have suggested techniques to support children with special needs but it is also worthwhile reading the whole of this book, as many of the points will apply and may be useful to you in supporting your child on the toilet training journey.

Children with special physical needs

For children with a physical disability, for example, cerebral
palsy or a spinal deformity, the process of toilet training often
takes longer. A child who has a physical disability may also
find undressing or getting to a potty or toilet more difficult. The
difficulties associated with wetting and soiling accidents can cause
enormous distress for the child and family.

In toilet training, the same principles apply to all children whether
they have a physical disability or not. As a parent you need to look
out for clues. Completing the 'Toilet readiness questionnaire' in
Chapter 2 may help you to identify the skills that your child has in
place. Let's recap on the signs of toilet readiness:

- ▶ *Your child can understand simple instructions such as 'Help
  me put your hat on'.*
- ▶ *Your child is able to sit on, and get up from, the potty with or
  without extra support. Seating aids are available; we will talk
  about this a little later on in the chapter.*
- ▶ *There is some evidence of regularity (especially of the bowel).*
- ▶ *Your child is beginning to recognize when she is wet or has
  done a poo.*
- ▶ *You feel that you and your child are ready to take on the task,
  so no major upheavals. Remember the list in Chapter 2 – when
  not to toilet train.*
- ▶ *Finally, and most importantly, you have the time available to
  develop a routine of regular toileting. Be aware that this may
  take some time and you may need to be quite regimented in
  your approach.*

You may find that you need to break down the steps of toilet
training into very small, achievable steps.

Before you start the toileting routine it may be helpful to keep a record
of your child's wetting and bowel habits. So, if you're noting when
your child has a poo, does it tend to happen at roughly the same time
each day? Does she have a bowel movement shortly after a mealtime?

And with bladder habits, are you becoming aware that your child
is holding on to a larger amount of urine before wetting her nappy?
(The nappy will feel suddenly full and warm if a large amount of
urine has been passed.)

Before starting the toileting routine, remember to think about
your child's fluid intake and diet. Go back and read Chapters 4
and 5. If your child does have any issues with constipation, then
this is the time to tackle the issue head-on. Seek advice from your
family doctor or a referral to an appropriate specialist such as a
paediatrician.

A routine for toileting

Start with bowel training, as this can often be easier as children
tend to open their bowels only once or twice a day and it is, of
course, easier to catch a poo.

Your record of when your child does a poo will help you to see
when she usually empties her bowels. This is often 20–40 minutes
after a meal, particularly after breakfast.

▶ *Encourage your child to stay on the toilet for five to ten
minutes; she may want to use an egg timer or an alarm clock
(this makes it fun). This may be the amount of time necessary
to empty the bowels so make sure she is not rushed, but do
not force her to sit for any longer.*

▶ *Make it a fun time – by reading a story, for example.*

▶ *Praise your child for sitting on the toilet, even if there are no results.*

▶ *The family may have to get up earlier than usual to ensure sufficient time for toileting. The aim is to give her time to relax and not to feel rushed before nursery or school.*

▶ *You may find it helpful to set up a reward scheme. Think about a star chart – Chapter 3 has details about how to set one up.*

If you are finding bowel training difficult or if your child needs specially adapted equipment in the home, your family doctor or hospital specialist may suggest that other health professionals are consulted. For example:

▶ *An occupational therapist from the Child Development Centre or social services may be helpful if the toilets at home or at the nursery or school need to be adapted. There are also special potty seats with harnesses and moulded seats available that can be placed over standard toilets. Ask for a referral and they will do an assessment of your child's needs.*

▶ *An occupational therapist from the Health Authority could help if your child is having difficulty using her hands or has co-ordination problems. The occupational therapist may have suggestions for improving your child's co-ordination or may be able to provide suitable equipment that will make the task easier.*

▶ *A physiotherapist may be able to give advice if your child needs help with, for example, transferring from a wheelchair to a toilet. The physiotherapist may be able to demonstrate how you can help your child onto the toilet.*

▶ *Many Child Development Centres have a specialist health visitor attached who may be able to give practical guidance and support with a toileting programme. Or she may be able to advise on suitable resources that could be useful.*

▶ *A dietician will be able to help if healthy eating is difficult to achieve, or if there is any concern about your child's diet.*

Bladder training

Before starting a bladder training routine, do make sure your child
is getting adequate fluids and is not constipated.

This is a regular, simple routine that may help your child achieve
daytime dryness.

WEEK ONE

Daily routine
On waking – remove your child's nappy and put her on the potty
or toilet as soon as possible. Toilet your child every one and a
quarter hours and keep a toileting diary. Remember there is a
suggested diary format in Chapter 4 that you can use. If accidents
do occur, try putting her on the potty or toilet every hour.

WEEK TWO

If your child is dry, with toileting every one to one and a quarter
hours, extend the time between visits to the toilet by 15 minutes
each time. If at the end of Week two there have been lots of
successes, then move to Week three. If your child is having lots of
accidents in Week two – stay at this toileting level until she is dry.

WEEK THREE

Extend the time again by 15 minutes to one and three quarter hours.

Continue to increase the time by 15 minutes each week until your
child can comfortably manage six visits to the toilet a day.

Where there are more complex causes of wetting and soiling accidents, it may be useful to gain the support of a continence adviser or clinical nurse specialist. Your family doctor or hospital specialist will be able to arrange a referral for you and your child.

If your child has a physical disability, with or without a learning difficulty, and has special educational needs, an assessment can be undertaken to provide support for your child when she starts school. A statement of special educational needs will outline your child's special needs and how they are to be met in school. For example, it should specify adaptations to the toilet and/or assistance with toileting. The process of obtaining a statement of special educational needs can take time to prepare so it is worth beginning the process early when, for example, your child is between the ages of two and three years.

Insight

Many parents or carers may need to 'toilet time' rather than 'toilet train' in the first instance, while helping the child to develop the skills needed for toilet training. This is simply getting into the routine of taking the child to the toilet every one to one and a half hours.

Learning disabilities

If your child has learning disabilities, whether moderate, severe or profound, the challenge as a parent is to work out the best approach at the most helpful time for your individual child.

Many children with more severe or profound learning disabilities may never be fully independent, but with the right advice and support (often requiring input from a range of health professionals), many children can become clean and dry without the need for nappies or pads.

Your child will need to be able to:

1 *recognize and understand the signals that she needs to 'go'*
2 *be able to wait until she reaches the toilet*
3 *manage her clothes*
4 *clean herself afterwards*
5 *flush the toilet and wash/dry her hands.*

For a child with learning difficulties these skills may be more difficult to master. She will need lots of practice and may need to have the skills broken down into little steps for her to master. Realistically, the process will probably take longer.

For some children with learning disabilities there will be a 'message processing' problem, with a difficulty in understanding or interpreting the signals from the bladder or bowel. You as the parent will need to help your child to learn to recognize the clues and signals.

Working out a programme

Consider what skills your child has. Using the 'Toilet readiness questionnaire' (Chapter 2) will help you to identify what skills your child already has.

Decide what you want to achieve, for example, do you expect your child to be fully independent or just to let you know when she needs to be taken to the toilet? This will depend very much on the type of learning disability your child has.

For some children, pictures or prompting by touch can be a way forward.

Children with autistic spectrum disorders often become very anxious when a routine is changed. Instructions using pictures or signs can help.

There are picture systems available, such as Widgit, the Picture Exchange Communication System (PECS) and Makaton – more details can be found on page 191 and in the 'Taking it further' section at the back of this book.

Again, keep a toileting diary for two to three weeks before starting your child's toileting routine. It will help you to decide the average intervals that your child goes between wees and when the most likely times are for emptying her bowels.

You may find that your child needs more incentives to sit on the potty or toilet, so make toilet training fun. Here are some suggestions:

- *A star chart with rewards – Chapter 3 outlines how to set one up.*
- *Jigsaw pieces – this is a fun way to encourage your child to sit on the potty or toilet. Your child is rewarded with a piece every time she sits on the potty or toilet. When the jigsaw is complete your child gets a treat.*
- *Another variation on the jigsaw puzzle theme is to have a picture of your child's favourite place or outing. Cut the picture into pieces (as many as you feel would be a manageable challenge for your child) – once the picture is complete the reward is a trip to the favourite place or outing.*
- *If your child enjoys music a musical potty may be the answer.*
- *Add food colouring to the water in the toilet – the idea is that she can flush the toilet only after doing a wee or poo.*
- *Sing a favourite song or rhyme while sitting on the toilet.*
- *An interest bag kept by the toilet may help your child sit for the required amount of time. Wrap up a valued object – for example, a favourite toy – and place in a bag. Use the idea of the bag to coax her to sit on the toilet. Let her have the bag and unwrap the object. This will act as a useful distraction – with the result that she stays on the toilet.*

If you are finding your child is reluctant to sit on the potty or toilet, break down the desired behaviour into tiny steps.

So, for example:

Step 1   Standing near the potty or toilet – give praise and
          reward.
Step 2   Sit on the potty or toilet with both clothes and nappy
          on – give praise and reward.
Step 3   Sit on the potty or toilet with a nappy on – give praise
          and reward.
Step 4   Sit on the potty or toilet without a nappy on – give praise
          and reward.
Step 5   Sit on potty or toilet and do a wee or poo – give praise
          and reward.

Do not move on to the next step until your child clearly feels
comfortable at each step and has had some success. It may take
some time to work through all the steps, but take it slowly and
keep positive.

Some children with learning disabilities may have difficulty with
sequencing. In this case, break down the desired behaviour into
small steps and reward the link between one action and another –
for example, going into the bathroom and switching on the light.
Reward the linking of the two actions and slowly build up the
sequence. You will need to make sure that you take your child
through the same routine each time. Again, using pictures to make
the routine clear can help. Use this sequence to help you:

▶ *Go to the bathroom.*
▶ *Turn on the light.*
▶ *Pull down my pants.*
▶ *Sit on the toilet.*
▶ *Use the toilet.*
▶ *Clean myself.*
▶ *Pull up my pants.*
▶ *Flush the toilet.*
▶ *Wash my hands.*
▶ *Turn out the light.*

Children with autistic spectrum disorders

Some children with autistic spectrum disorders – for example autism and Asperger's syndrome – may struggle with the routines of toilet training and have worries about what is expected of them. It is very difficult to know what will work for an individual child, but some of the following suggestions may be relevant to your child:

▶ *If your child has difficulty with making sense of the sequence of toileting, using pictures to illustrate the sequence may help.*

▶ *Think about whether your child feels comfortable and safe in the bathroom. Is the toilet at the right height for her or do you need to think about a step? Will she be happier using a potty rather than a toilet? You know your child best and will be in tune with what will cause anxiety for her and can tailor your approach to suit.*

▶ *Some children are upset by noise and may be frightened by the toilet being flushed. If your child is sensitive to noise then wait until she leaves the bathroom before flushing the toilet.*

▶ *Making toileting more interesting can be a help, so the idea of a ping pong ball floating in the toilet may appeal to boys who are learning to wee standing up to help with their aim. Also colour can give the variety your child needs. Different food colourings can be used to colour the toilet water. Your child may have a favourite or may like to choose.*

These ideas are to encourage your child to use the toilet.

Other resources

There are a number of websites and organizations that you may find helpful:

ERIC – Education and Resources for Improving Childhood Continence.

ERIC sells a range of literature for children, teenagers and parents on bedwetting, daytime wetting and soiling. They also have a range of literature for children with special needs. A wide range of associated resources is also available, for example, enuresis alarms and bedding protection. If you go to the website you will find an online shop for purchasing resources. There is also a helpline for parents.

ERIC Helpline 0845 370 8008, Monday to Friday, from 10 a.m. to 4 p.m.

ERIC website – www.eric.org.uk

Widgit – a system using symbols to help those with physical and/or learning disabilities to communicate with their parents or carers.

Widgit website – www.widgit.com

The Picture Exchange Communication System (PECS) – this helps children and adults with autistic spectrum disorders express their needs to a parent or carer.

PECS website – www.pecs.org.uk

Do2Learn – this website uses pictures to help children to sequence a routine. They have a specific resource for toileting and lots of other ideas.

Do2Learn website – www.do2learn.com

The EarlyBird programme – organized by the National Autistic Society is a course for parents and carers for children under five.

Website – www.nas.org.uk/earlybird

Makaton – this is a language programme made up of signs and symbols to teach communication skills.

Website – www.makaton.org

Contact a Family – a UK-based charity that provides advice, information and support for parents of all disabled children, no matter what their disability or health condition. The charity has a message forum for parents to communicate with one another and is able to link one family with another family that has a child with the same condition. Parents can gain a huge amount of support from another family in the same situation.

Website – www.cafamily.org.uk

> **Insight**
>
> Don't forget about the range of health-care professionals who can help and support you and your child during toilet training.

Summary

For some children with special needs, acquiring toileting skills will be a challenge. You as parents will know your child best and will be aware of what might work for her. This chapter has outlined some general ideas on how you may be able to help your child to achieve bowel and bladder control. Don't forget you are not alone and there is a whole host of health professionals out there to offer you support and advice on resources that are available.

10 THINGS TO REMEMBER

1 *Children with special needs will need the same skills in place that we have talked about in previous chapters – but it may be that these skills will take longer to learn.*

2 *Do use the toilet readiness questionnaire – it will help you to identify the areas where your child needs extra support.*

3 *Remember that bowel training is often easier than bladder training, especially if your child has regular bowel movements.*

4 *You will need to be very organized about a toileting routine.*

5 *For some children a visual or physical prompt can be helpful. These can reinforce the messages that you are communicating to your child.*

6 *Don't forget that incentives can work really well.*

7 *If your child has difficulty with sequencing, breaking down the routine into small steps with a reward at the end of each step may be the way forward.*

8 *There are lots of organizations that may be able to help and they often have many useful resources.*

9 *Don't forget the health professionals who are involved with your child's care. They usually have a lot of experience in this area and will be able to help you.*

10 *Use the resources offered by the internet – you may be surprised by just how much information, help and support is out there.*

11

11

Medical conditions

In this chapter you will learn about:
- *urinary tract infections*
- *daytime wetting*
- *vesico-ureteric reflux (VUR)*.

There are a number of medical conditions that can affect the urinary tract and these can have an impact on toilet training. In this chapter we will look at the most common of these conditions that you may come across.

Urinary tract infections in children

Urinary tract infections affect about three per cent of children every year – and about twice as many girls as boys are affected in this way. It can sometimes be very difficult, especially in younger children, to be sure that what you are dealing with is a urinary tract infection. The symptoms are not always obvious and younger children are usually unable to describe how they feel in the depth of detail that you would need to make a diagnosis possible. However, recognizing the symptoms quickly would allow your child to be promptly treated so it is worthwhile learning a bit about urinary tract infections so that you know what to look out for. Untreated urinary tract infections can lead to serious kidney problems and could also lead to high blood pressure in later life.

How does the urinary tract normally function?

Everyone has two kidneys, which filter and remove waste and water from the blood to produce urine. The urine then travels from the kidneys down two narrow tubes (ureters), where it is then stored in a balloon-shaped organ called the bladder.

In a child, the bladder can hold about 30–45 ml of urine for each year of a child's age, so the bladder of a four-year-old child will hold about 120–180 ml, and an eight-year-old can hold about 240–360 ml. When the bladder empties, a muscle called the sphincter relaxes and urine flows out of the body through the urethra, a tube at the bottom of the bladder.

The opening of the urethra is at the end of the penis in boys and in front of the vagina in girls.

How does the urinary tract become infected?

Normal urine contains no bacteria (germs) – in fact it is sterile. However, bacteria may at times get into the urinary tract and into the urine (from the skin around the rectum and the genitals) by travelling up the urethra into the bladder. When this happens, the bacteria can infect and inflame the bladder causing swelling and pain in the lower tummy. This is what is known as a bladder infection.

If the bacteria travel up through the ureters to the kidneys, a kidney infection can develop. Kidney infections are much more serious than bladder infections.

In some children a urinary tract infection may be a sign of an abnormal urinary tract that may be prone to repeated problems. For this reason when a child has a urinary tract infection, additional tests or investigations are often recommended.

> **Insight**
> Girls have a much shorter urethra than boys (the tube running from the bladder to the outside), so they are more likely to get an infection.

What are the symptoms of a urinary tract infection?

If we look at an infection of the bladder first, the symptoms that you would look for are:

▶ *pain or burning sensation on doing a wee*
▶ *needing to wee more frequently or urgently*
▶ *cloudy, blood-stained or foul-smelling urine*
▶ *pain in the lower tummy*
▶ *mild fever, i.e. 37–38.3°C.*

A kidney infection may produce all the same symptoms as a bladder infection but with additional symptoms, including:

▶ *a higher fever, i.e. over 38.3°C*
▶ *nausea and/or vomiting*
▶ *shaking and chills*
▶ *pain in the back or in the side.*

How to test for a urinary tract infection

If you think your child has an infection it is important that they are seen by a GP as soon as possible. They will want to test your child's urine and exactly how they do this will depend on your child's age. If your child is toilet trained it will simply be a case of your child weeing into a container – which will be supplied by your doctor. For a younger child, a plastic collection bag may be placed over the genital area. It will be sealed to the skin with an adhesive strip and then it is a matter of waiting for the next wee. The wee will be decanted from the plastic bag into a container again supplied by your GP. The urine will then be sent to the local hospital to test for bacteria (germs).

Insight

Urinary tract infections can often be difficult to diagnose. If you're unsure it is always worth a trip to the GP to ask for a urine test.

Treatment

The usual treatment for any infection is oral antibiotics. However, a urine sample needs to be obtained before the antibiotics are started. The urine will be tested for bacteria and occasionally, depending on the bacteria found, there might need to be a change of antibiotics – but your GP will advise you.

If your child is given antibiotics it is very important to complete the course so that the infection is truly cleared up. Often children respond very quickly to antibiotics and can seem much better after a day or two, and it is tempting to think that the infection has gone. But it may not have, so you must complete the course to make sure that the infection has completely cleared.

You will also be told to make sure your child is drinking plenty again (remember: six to eight small drinks of about 150 ml each). If you have an older child they will be able to manage more fluid. In this situation, if at all possible, try to encourage them to drink more. One way is to keep reminding them to have sips of water and for them to have a drink close by at all times.

Your doctor will advise on paracetamol or Nurofen for any pain that your child is experiencing and also to help bring their temperature down. It is important that you follow the manufacturers' instructions on how much and how often to give your child paracetamol or Nurofen – it will be clearly labelled on the packaging.

Further tests

If your child has had a urinary tract infection it is likely that further tests or investigations will be recommended. Your GP will refer your child to a paediatrician (children's doctor) at your local hospital. The tests that are advised may depend on your local hospital's policies and the child's age. They will, however, usually include the following:

1 **An ultrasound scan (US scan).** *This test does not involve any injections or X-rays, just some cold gel on your child's stomach and back. It enables the outline of the kidneys, tubes and bladder to be seen on a screen.*
2 **A bladder X-ray.** *The other test that may be advised for young children is a bladder X-ray with the complicated-sounding name of a 'micturating cysto-urethrogram'. This test will check for an abnormality of the bladder or weakness of the tubes leading back from the bladder to the kidneys (this abnormality is known as vesico-ureteric reflux – or reflux for short – see below). This test does involve X-rays and also the injection of a dye through a small tube (a catheter), which is passed up the urethra into the bladder.*

If your child has suffered a urinary tract infection your GP may prescribe a daily low dose of antibiotics after the original course of antibiotics has finished while your child is waiting to have these tests done. The aim is to prevent a further urine infection from occurring before the results of any tests are known. It is important to remember that in many cases the results will be normal and it is quite possible that your child may never have a urinary tract infection again.

How to prevent a urinary tract infection

Top tips

- *Deal with constipation – children with severe constipation are more prone to urine infections. This is because large hard stools sometimes collect in the rectum (back passage) and press on the bladder. The bladder may not empty fully when the child passes urine, which can make the urine more prone to becoming infected. Treating severe constipation sometimes prevents recurring urine infections.*
- *Make sure your child is drinking enough. A minimum of six to eight small drinks of 150 ml each spread out over the day is advisable.*
- *Encourage your child to empty his bladder every two hours.*
- *In young girls it is important to avoid any irritants in the vaginal area. Some bubble baths and soaps can cause irritation. Avoid these and, if using soap, go for a pure, simple, unperfumed, vegetable-based soap.*
- *Teach girls how to clean themselves correctly after going to the toilet – from front to back – so that bacteria are not transferred from the anus to the urethra.*
- *Buy loose cotton pants for your child – never use nylon ones.*
- *With boys the foreskin may be a source of infection so make sure this is kept clean.*

A parent's experience

Priya was two years and three months old when she had a kidney infection.

She had been unwell for a couple of days – out of sorts with a bit of a temperature. After a couple of days, I took her to the doctor's. He checked her all over and said it was

(Contd)

probably a virus. He said to give her Calpol to bring her temperature down and to bring her back again in two days if there was no improvement. She seemed to perk up the day after, so I thought she must have been beginning to get over whatever it was. But on the fourth day she woke up with a really high temperature of 39°C and complaining of tummy ache. She would not eat or drink anything and just kept crying. I started to get really worried about her and managed to get an emergency appointment for her at the end of the morning surgery.

By the time we got to the doctor's her temperature was up to 39.5°C, she had had Calpol but it had not brought her temperature down. The GP checked her all over again, her ears, chest and throat, but everything was clear. He then said it might be a urinary tract infection and, because her temperature was so high, that she should be seen at the local hospital. He gave us a letter to take to casualty and he phoned ahead to let them know we were on our way. Priya was getting a bit sleepy by now and slept all the way there.

The casualty department staff were great when we arrived – as soon as we checked in at reception we were taken straight through to the children's area. A nurse took Priya's temperature and it was still 39.5°C, so she was given another dose of Calpol. They said they needed to get a urine sample. Priya was still in nappies so they put a plastic bag with an adhesive strip on her to catch a wee. In the meantime a doctor came to see her. The doctor said it was probably a urinary tract infection and because her tummy and now her back were hurting, and with such a high temperature, it was likely that it was a kidney infection. The doctor said she needed antibiotics but could not start them until we had a wee sample from her. We had to try and keep giving her sips of water. While they were waiting for her to do a wee, it was decided to put a drip up and to give her some fluids that way. They also took some blood. I was really scared when they said they needed to take blood and put a drip in, but they used magic cream (as they called it) to numb the skin so when they put the needle in it did not hurt her. Eventually she did a wee and when they tested it, it had loads of protein and blood in it. A senior doctor came and saw us then and said that Priya had a suspected kidney infection and that it was serious. She would need to stay in hospital for a few days and have intravenous antibiotics to get rid of the infection. They gave her her first dose of antibiotics in casualty and then took us up to the children's ward. All the staff were fantastic and really took good care of us. My husband and I took it in turns to stay with Priya and we had a camp bed at the bottom of her cot at night-time.

The antibiotics worked brilliantly and by the next day her temperature was beginning to come down and she was not complaining of tummy ache or backache as much. The doctors were really pleased with her progress. She stayed in hospital for four days in all and was discharged with oral antibiotics.

Before we left the hospital, the consultant came to see us and said that because it was such a serious infection they needed to do some more tests to check that her kidneys had not been damaged. This would also help them to discover if there was a reason as to why she had got the infection in the first place. We were told that she needed to be on a small daily dose of antibiotics until the tests had been done to prevent a further infection from happening – within a week she was back to her old self.

We went back for the tests about a month after she was discharged from hospital. She had an ultrasound of her kidneys and bladder. She thought that was quite funny and said it tickled. She also had an X-ray of her kidneys and bladder. They had to put a catheter into her bladder. It was not very pleasant, but we managed. The good news was that no damage had occurred as a result of the infection. Also the X-ray was normal.

(Contd)

When the results of the urine test came back, it showed that the infection was caused by bacteria called *E. coli*. The consultant told us that *E. coli* is in the bowel and can be passed via poo. She said it would be a really good idea to toilet train Priya sooner rather than later. We were also told to make sure she had plenty to drink, not allow her to get constipated and not to use bubble bath. We were advised that whenever she got a high temperature her urine should be tested. We did everything that we were told to do. I was paranoid for a while after and if ever she was unwell or had a slight temperature I rushed her off to the GP. She is six now and in Year 1 at school. She has never had another urinary tract infection.

Daytime wetting

Daytime wetting is when a child over the age of five years is regularly wetting his pants during the day. We are not talking about the odd accident, which can still be common at this age – especially if your child has started school recently. Here, we're looking at when it is happening on a regular basis. This might be once or twice a week or it may be a daily occurrence. The amount of urine may vary from just a little damp patch on the pants to noticeable wetness of clothes.

In some cases daytime wetting will be due to a delay in toilet training and will just sort itself out in time. But for some children there may be a problem with the way in which the bladder is working. Some children have what is called an irritable bladder, which can give them a sudden urge to wee, and they may need to wee more frequently than other children. Children who have daytime wetness due to an irritable bladder are also more likely to take longer to acquire night-time dryness. In a very small number of cases a child may have a smaller than normal bladder capacity. If your child is still wetting after the age of four or five years it is advisable to see your GP for advice.

A parent's experience

Lucy was three years old when it became apparent that there were issues with toilet training. All of her friends – both boys and girls – were out of nappies in the day and although some still had accidents they were pretty much dry. Lucy could not seem to hold on to her wee for more than about 15 minutes. We had tried on a number of occasions to train her, but to no avail. I decided that I was going to talk to my health visitor about it.

I half expected her to say 'Don't worry about it, she will do it when she is ready', but she didn't. She really listened to what I said and asked loads of questions about her understanding and speech. We then spent quite a while talking about what happened when Lucy did not have a nappy on. Often she would do a wee and then 10–15 minutes later dash to the potty again but it would be too late. The health visitor felt that Lucy did have the understanding and skills necessary for control but that maybe there was something wrong with her bladder. She suggested that we saw our GP and that the first step should be to have her urine tested for an infection. She said it sounded unlikely to be an infection as there were no other signs and she was in good health, but that this needed to be excluded. Then, if there was no infection present, our GP may decide to refer her to a paediatrician. I was upset at the thought that there may be something wrong but also relieved that I had been taken seriously and not labelled a fussy mother. I found it really helped to talk it through with someone who was not closely involved.

My GP agreed with what the health visitor had said. The urine test came back negative so then Lucy was referred to a paediatrician. We had to wait six weeks for the

(Contd)

appointment. The paediatrician listened to what we had to say and agreed that there could well be something wrong with Lucy's bladder. Lucy had to have a number of tests and we found out that she had a smaller than normal bladder, which was also irritable. We were told that she would need medication to stop the bladder from being irritable and, because her bladder was small, we would need to train her to go to the toilet on a regular basis. The medication really helped, and she is now able to hold on to her wee for about an hour and a half. She is out of nappies in the day and most days she is accident-free, but we have to be really disciplined about her going to the toilet on a regular basis. She is due to start school soon and I am feeling very anxious about how she will get on, but we have been in to talk to the head teacher and the reception class teacher about how we will manage the situation and we came away feeling positive. Her bladder is growing, although it is still small. The hospital are really pleased with her progress and have said that, in time, she will be able to come off the medication.

Vesico-ureteric reflux (VUR)

This occurs when the valve between the ureters and the bladder is not working properly, allowing urine to flow backwards into the ureters. Depending on the severity of the problem, the urine can flow back to the kidney resulting in an infection.

Insight
Be reassured that most children will have grown out of the condition of vesico-ureteric reflux by the age of five.

SIGNS AND SYMPTOMS

Before birth
Vesico-ureteric reflux is often picked up on an ultrasound scan when the baby is still in the womb. When this happens the baby will be started on a small dose of daily antibiotics after the birth, and further investigations will be done.

After a urinary tract infection
Vesico-ureteric reflux is sometimes found when a child has suffered a urinary tract infection and has had further tests done.

TESTS

A child will have an ultrasound scan and a micturating cysto-urethrogram (as described in the section above about urinary tract infection) in order to detect the problem.

There are five grades of vesico-ureteric reflux. These range from Grade One, where the urine flows back up the ureters but not to the kidney, to Grade Five, where the urine flows all the way back to the kidneys. One or both kidneys can be affected.

HOW COMMON IS VUR?

About one in 1000 children is affected and it is more common in girls. If one child in the family has it, other siblings should be monitored for it, as there is an increased risk that they may be affected.

TREATMENT

A child with this condition will be treated with a low dose of daily antibiotics to prevent a urinary tract infection. The treatment may continue until the age of five and the child will need regular urine tests.

The really good news is that when this condition is picked up early and the child receives treatment, permanent damage to the kidney can be prevented. Also, reassuringly, children often outgrow this condition by the age of five years.

A parent's experience

When we went for our scan for Charlie when I was pregnant, we were devastated to be told that there was something wrong with the tubes that lead up to his kidneys. They called it reflux and said that when he was born he would need further tests and would have to take antibiotics possibly until he started school. This is not what we expected to hear; Charlie was our first child and we had just expected that everything would be fine. We were told that he would be seen by a paediatrician after he was born and would be started on antibiotics. He would also have to come back into hospital when he was a few weeks old for further tests.

When he was born we were overjoyed – he was our perfect little boy. He did his first wee soon after he was born and the paediatrician who came to see us was very reassuring as he told us that, with treatment, hopefully everything would be fine and he said children usually grow out of reflux by the time they start school.

We left hospital with Charlie's antibiotics, feeling a little better. But that's when the problems started. I found it really difficult to get Charlie to take the antibiotic – he just did not like the taste. Also, I was really stressed at the thought of the tests that he would have to go through; it all seemed so unfair.

I was having a really bad day and I think I had a severe bout of the baby blues when the health visitor called to see Charlie and me. I broke down in a terrible state and it all came flooding out. The first thing my health visitor did after mopping up the tears and making us both a cup of tea was to show me a couple of really simple techniques for getting the medicine down Charlie. It worked like magic and Charlie

206

took the antibiotics without a fuss. The next thing she did was to suggest putting us in touch with another family who had an older child with the same condition. That way I could find out first-hand not only what it would be like for Charlie to have the tests but also how things were progressing for them. She was really upbeat about the whole thing and said that she had come across a number of children with this condition and they had all done fine. She went away and arranged for the other mum to contact me. Sandra called a couple of days later and suggested I go around there for coffee. Her son, Alfie, was 18 months and the same thing had happened to them – the reflux had been picked up on a scan while Sandra was pregnant. She talked me through the tests and what they had done. Alfie was also taking daily antibiotics and Sandra said he was doing fine. He had had no infections and the doctors were really delighted with his progress.

Eventually, Charlie had the tests done and it was confirmed that he had reflux. He is now two and a half and out of nappies and he also has had no infections. I am pregnant with my second child and they have just done a scan and said that it looks like this baby is not affected by the condition, which is great news.

I really think for us it made a big difference being able to talk to other parents who had been through what we were going through.

Frequently asked questions

Q1: *My daughter has had a wee infection. The hospital has done some tests and said everything is normal. But I am worried about it happening again and I know that she does not drink much at school. Is there anything I can do to prevent it happening again?*

That is great news that all the hospital tests came back normal. To prevent another infection you need to make sure your daughter is drinking enough fluids throughout the day and that she has a regular toileting routine. Encourage her to go to the toilet every two hours so that her bladder is regularly emptied. Make sure she has a drink before leaving for school and ask her teacher if she can bring in a water bottle with her to drink throughout the day. Remind her to have a drink at lunchtime and another as soon as she gets in from school. If there are any issues with constipation, make sure you sort these out and check that she knows how to wipe herself after she has been to the toilet.

Q2: *I know it is important to make sure children drink plenty of fluids but, honestly, my kids are a nightmare – they barely have a couple of glasses of fluid a day. What can I do?*

There are other ways of giving a child fluids other than drinks. Think about sugar-free jelly for dessert and diluted fruit juice lollies that you can make at home. Also custard and rice pudding are other ways to increase fluid intake. Take your children shopping and have a look at the lovely character water bottles that are on the market. Fill them up with tap water and have them on hand and encourage them to take regular sips of water – it soon adds up.

Summary

This chapter has highlighted the most common medical conditions that can affect the urinary tract and have an impact on toilet training. The take-home message has to be that if a medical condition is picked up early and treated promptly, further damage can be prevented.

10 THINGS TO REMEMBER

1 *Urinary tract infections affect about three per cent of children a year, so they are not that uncommon.*

2 *Girls are more prone to these infections so remember to teach girls to wipe from front to back.*

3 *Remember what the symptoms are – pain or burning sensation on doing a wee, needing to wee more frequently or urgently, cloudy, blood-stained or foul-smelling urine, pain in the lower tummy and a mild fever, i.e. 37–38°C.*

4 *Always seek medical attention if you suspect that your child has a urinary tract infection.*

5 *A urinary specimen is usually needed before antibiotics can be started.*

6 *Your child may need some simple tests to see if he has a urinary tract infection.*

7 *Remember the top tips to help prevent an infection – deal with constipation, ensure the child is drinking plenty and emptying his bladder every two hours or so, avoid irritants such as strong soaps, encourage girls to wipe from front to back, use cotton pants and keep boys' foreskins clean.*

8 *If your child is still experiencing daytime wetting at the age of four to five, it is advisable to see your GP.*

9 *Vesico-ureteric reflux is often picked up on an ultrasound scan when a baby is in the womb, but it is also sometimes diagnosed after a child has had a urinary tract infection.*

10 *Children often grow out of this condition by the age of five.*

12

....

Special situations

In this chapter you will learn:
- *some of the situations that can impact on toilet training*
- *how to deal with these situations*
- *top tips to help you cope.*

Life has its ups and downs for all of us and, just as we adults can have our stressful times, so can young children. Often, very young children, who perhaps have not yet begun to use verbal communication or are just beginning to do so, find that the only way to get the message across to us that they are unhappy is by their behaviour. It is not uncommon for there to be a regression in a child's behaviour when there has been a major life change, for example, a new baby in the family or a house move. But there can also be a change in behaviour when children are simply out of their normal routine. These changes in behaviour often involve children's toilet habits, as this is one area where they can exert some control. Or maybe they feel upset and simply forget to use the potty or the toilet.

Let's look at some of these situations and how you can deal with them:

New baby in the family

This is probably the most stressful change that can happen to a child – a new sibling in the family. Having said that, it is very natural and also healthy for your child to react if she is in this situation.

Just try to imagine yourself in your child's situation. How would you feel if your partner came home from work one day and said that someone new was going to move in with you and share your bedroom!? Not only that, but this new person was going to need lots of attention and plenty of time spent with her. What if your partner also told you that all your favourite relatives and friends would come to visit this new person and would bring lots of presents for her? Also, best of all, that this new person was going to stay forever and that you would have to learn to share with this new person. What child would not be a little put out at having a new sibling? Some sort of reaction is almost inevitable.

It will depend very much at what age your child is when the new sibling arrives as to how she will react. It is quite common for children who were previously dry to start wetting themselves when there is a new baby in the family. Of course, this is, without a doubt, the best way to get attention from a very tired set of parents. If you find that this is happening, go back to the golden rule – never get cross or show your child that you are upset by this behaviour. Ignore it, clean her up and change her. Then look at ways to build up her self-confidence again by praising all positive behaviour and ignoring, where possible, all negative behaviour. Using a star chart with some small tasks may be a good incentive and, when she has got the hang of the star chart, add being dry to it.

Below are some top tips for helping to make the passage of having a new sibling in the family a little easier for your child to accept. Mostly, it's a case of making your child feel involved in what is happening to the family and of building up her confidence.

Top tips to help you cope

▶ *Prepare your child in plenty of time before the new baby arrives. Talk to her about what it will be like when the baby comes. If possible take her to a scan appointment*

(Contd)

so she can make sense of the situation and to a midwife's check so that your child can hear the baby's heartbeat (children love being able to do this).

▶ Think about buying a special present for the baby to give your older child and vice versa – let your child choose a present to give to the baby.

▶ Have childcare plans in place for when mum goes into labour. Make sure your child knows who will be looking after her and where.

▶ It is not a good idea to toilet train just before or just after the arrival of a new baby.

▶ If the new baby will be using the older sibling's cot and she is still in the cot, arrange to move her to a bed well before the baby is due. It is important that she doesn't feel displaced.

▶ There are lots of lovely books on the market about new babies in the family. Here is a suggested list:

  ▷ Waiting for Baby (All Day Long) – by Frank Endersby [Child's Play (International) Ltd].

  ▷ I'm a Big Brother and I'm a Big Sister – both by Joanne Cole (Eos).

  ▷ I Want a Sister (a Little Princess Story) – by Tony Ross (Harper Collins).

▶ Once the baby is born, make sure siblings get to hold the baby before other family members (except mum and dad of course).

▶ Give your child little jobs to do to help her feel important – like helping with nappy changing or bathing.

▶ Children often feel displaced when a new baby arrives. It is normal and healthy for them to feel cross or sad about the situation. They often take their feelings out on their parents rather than the baby. It will pass.

▶ Where possible, keep existing routines in place. Young children thrive on routines and when there is a new baby in the family it can make them feel more secure if their routines are not altered.

▶ Tell your child how grown up she is and what a great help she is to you. But don't forget that before the new baby was born she was your baby and sometimes she may want to be your baby again.

▶ When visitors come to see the new baby, if the older sibling is present, encourage the visitors not to make too much of a fuss of the new baby.

▶ It is now quite fashionable for visitors to bring a present for the baby and for other siblings too, which is lovely. If there is no present for the older child, be discreet about the baby's present – maybe open it later when the older child has gone to bed.

▶ Try and arrange at some stage in the day to have some time alone with the older child when the baby is sleeping and do an activity together – read a book or play a game.

▶ In the evenings try to make sure that your child again has some time alone with you or your partner. Maybe at bedtime you can read stories and chat about the day.

▶ At the weekends, if both parents are around, try to arrange a little outing with one of the parents and the older child only. It can be something simple such as a trip to the park or maybe a swim.

▶ Children often regress in some area of their development when a new baby is born. They may start wetting. This is not uncommon. Stay calm, don't get upset or cross. Just clean your child up and get on with life. Consider using a star chart to get your child back on track.

▶ If possible, avoid any other major life change for your child when a new baby arrives. For example, try not to start a new playgroup/nursery or move house.

A parent's experience

Tyler was four years old when her new baby brother came along. We had gone to great lengths to prepare her, but even so she reacted badly. She was fine for the first two or three weeks – she really liked all the attention that she was getting

(Contd)

and the presents. Then we needed to get back into the old routine of nursery and just generally getting on with stuff. That was when it all started to fall apart. Tyler did not like the idea that she went off to nursery while I stayed at home with the baby. She wanted to stay at home with us as she thought she was missing out. She started wetting at nursery during the second week that she was back. I think she thought that maybe if she had lots of accidents at nursery then I would not send her. I had a long chat with the nursery teacher and we agreed that we needed to ride this one out. She suggested a star chart with stickers at home as well as at nursery with lots of praise, and we were not to react to the wetting. I also started to talk to Tyler about all the boring things that I did when she went to nursery and I went home, like the washing and the ironing. She began to realize that her brother was asleep and that being at nursery was much more exciting than being at home. It took a couple of weeks, but we got there.

Illness

Another situation that can cause behavioural problems is illness. It is not uncommon when children become ill for them to regress to some extent with toileting. Sometimes, day- or night-wetting when a child has previously been dry may, in itself, be a sign that your child is unwell. It can sometimes be a sign of a urinary tract infection so it is worth talking to your GP and asking to have your child's urine tested.

When a child has been successfully dry and then falls ill and begins to wet, it is tempting to put her back into nappies for convenience's sake. This can be counterproductive and may result in needing to go through the toilet training process all over again. It is much better to just accept the situation, empathize with your child and make sure you encourage her to use the potty or toilet on a more regular basis. The situation will pass. Your child is not doing it on purpose.

Top tips to help you cope

▶ *If your child is unwell and starts wetting, always have her urine checked for an infection.*

▶ *If the urine is not infected, she may be wetting because she is dehydrated and the urine is concentrated. Concentrated urine can cause the bladder to become irritated and the child may wet. Make sure your child is getting plenty to drink – at least six to eight drinks each day, more if you can manage it. Have a water bottle close by and encourage sips of water all day.*

▶ *Make sure you take your child to the toilet on a regular basis, you may need to go back to once every hour or once every hour and a half.*

▶ *Keep a potty close by.*

▶ *Praise your child every time she uses the potty or toilet.*

▶ *Remember, don't get cross if she has an accident – it is not her fault.*

A parent's experience

William (three years and six months) was out of nappies early, just after his second birthday, but every time he is unwell he starts to wet himself again. It is usually the day before he comes down with whatever it is and then for the first day of the illness. Now we realize that if he wets then it is likely that he is going to be unwell. It is a bit like a warning sign. I have had a chat with my GP about it and he has given us a supply of urine bottles, just so that he can check his urine in case it is an infection. It never has been a urinary tract infection but we still always get it checked. The GP thinks he will grow out of it. It does seem to be less common now than it was when he was younger.

Moving house

Moving house is a huge upheaval for all of us. Imagine what it must be like for a small child. She may well be moving from the very first – and only – home that she has known. She may not have considered that you would, or could, live anywhere else. It can be a difficult concept for young children to take on board. Moving house can also mean lots of other things happen like having to go to a new playgroup, nursery or school. There may also be new friends and neighbours. Their rooms will be different and all their possessions may be in different places in the new home. It is a lot to deal with and it would be quite reasonable for a child to display some negative behaviour. Here again is a list of top tips that can help you deal with your child during a house move.

Top tips to help you cope

- *Let your child see your new home before you move and make sure she knows where she will sleep.*
- *Where possible include your child in your plans and let her be involved in discussions about the new home.*
- *Let your child help with the packing. Especially her toys and clothes.*
- *When packing, discuss with your child what special toys she wants to take in the car. Pack a separate bag with her favourite pyjamas, cup, bottle and comfort object for the first night.*
- *Discuss with your child what will happen on the day of the move. Where will she be? Will she be at home or at nursery or school? When will she see her new home?*
- *If possible, concentrate on getting her bedroom with bedding, toys, books and clothes sorted out first.*
- *If you are planning on decorating your child's room, let her help you to choose the colour for the walls and maybe bedding or curtains or blinds. Again, this gives her a sense of ownership.*
- *Make sure your child knows where the bathroom is and is familiar with the layout of the new home.*

- ▶ If your child is still using a potty, make sure it is on hand and that she knows where it is.
- ▶ Try, wherever possible, to keep routines in place.
- ▶ For the first few days after moving it is nice to give your child some time pottering around her new home so she can start to feel comfortable.
- ▶ Your child may want to talk about how much she misses her old home so give her the opportunity and try to empathize with her.

A parent's experience

We moved house when the girls were six and eight years old. On the day of moving we arranged for their grandparents to collect them from school and for them to stay with them for the weekend. Before the move they had done this on a regular basis, so they were quite happy with the arrangements. We then spent the next two days unpacking and getting everything we could in place. We concentrated really hard on the girls' bedrooms so that by the time we went to collect them on the Sunday evening their rooms were all unpacked and arranged as they had been at the old house. We both felt this really helped the girls to settle in quickly and also allowed us to do most of the unpacking without those helpful hands!

Starting nursery or school

Starting nursery or school is a major event in any child's life. It is the beginning of the real journey to independence for your child and is a time of letting go for parents. During the first few days and weeks of starting nursery or school, your child will be exposed to a new environment, with new people to get to know and new rules to learn and follow. This is a daunting prospect for even the most confident of children. Again, wetting really is not uncommon in the early days of this new experience and is completely understandable. Help your child to overcome this type of situation by ensuring that she is confident in her toileting before starting nursery or playgroup if at all possible. Being reliably dry and clean during the day means:

▶ *knowing when she needs the toilet and responding to that need straight away*
▶ *being able to communicate effectively that she needs to go to the toilet*
▶ *when she reaches the toilet, being able to pull down her clothes and pull them up again*
▶ *being able to clean herself after a wee or a poo*
▶ *knowing how to wash her hands thoroughly and always doing it.*
▶ *If your child is starting nursery or school, try following these top tips for helping her to settle into this new and exciting environment.*

Top tips to help you cope

▶ *Arrange for your child to visit her new nursery or school in advance. Let her have a good look around and explain to her the different areas and what happens there. Talk to her about where she will put her coat (find her peg) and show her various important areas such as the toilets, playground, garden, dining room, hall and so on depending on the type of premises that she is going to be attending.*
▶ *If possible, introduce her to her key worker if at nursery, or class teacher if at school.*
▶ *In the weeks before she starts nursery or school, whenever you pass the building, point it out to your child and talk about it.*
▶ *Talk about what you liked about going to nursery or school when you were her age and, if possible, get older siblings involved in the discussion.*
▶ *There are some lovely books on the market about starting nursery and school. The following are just two of them, but if*

*you visit the library or any good children's bookshop you will
find a host of titles to choose from:*

  ▷ Topsy and Tim Start School *by Jean and Gareth
  Adamson (Ladybird Books Ltd).*
  ▷ Starting School *by Alan and Janet Ahlberg (Picture Puffin).*

▶ *Talk about the settling-in period and how it will be for her.*
▶ *If she is staying for lunch, describe to her what that will be like.*
▶ *If your child needs a uniform, make sure you get it in plenty of
time and that she has had an opportunity to try it all on before
her first day.*
▶ *Taking a photograph of your child in her uniform on the first
day of nursery or school is a nice way to mark the occasion.*
▶ *Talk to your child about how to ask to go to the toilet. A
session of role-play often works wonders in this situation,
especially for children who are starting school and may feel
nervous about asking.*
▶ *If there is no uniform make sure that whatever clothing she is
wearing is easy for her to deal with when she needs to go to
the toilet. So, no difficult buttons or dungarees.*
▶ *Encourage her to learn to dress and undress herself and, if she
is starting school, make sure that she knows how to wipe her
bottom.*
▶ *It is a nice idea, if possible, for your child to have a play date
with another child who will be starting nursery or school at
the same time as her. Then, on her first day there will be at
least one familiar face.*
▶ *An early night combined with a good night's sleep before your
child's first day is a must.*
▶ *A nutritious breakfast and a drink before leaving home will
help your child to enjoy every nursery or school day.*
▶ *Getting to nursery or school on time means that your child
won't miss any important instructions first thing.*
▶ *Do be a little early to collect her. Children get very anxious if
they see all their friends going off with their parents and they
appear to be left behind.*
▶ *Give your child time to talk about her day and listen carefully.*
▶ *A snack at the end of the nursery or school day is helpful to
boost those energy levels.*

Holidays

Holidays are great fun but the getting there can be quite stressful and the routine of your child's day will undoubtedly be changed. When you have a newly toilet trained child you need to do a bit of forward planning to help ease the journey.

Top tips for the journey

▶ *Plan the route that you will take and make sure you schedule in sufficient stops.*

▶ *Be prepared for the journey to take longer, as you will need to stop more frequently.*

▶ *Before you set off make sure your child has had the opportunity to have a wee and a poo if need be.*

▶ *If you think there is a risk of an accident, protect the car seat with a disposable mat (we have mentioned these in earlier chapters).*

▶ *Have spare clothes at the ready and some wipes available just in case.*

▶ *Do not restrict fluids, as this can cause the urine to become concentrated. This, in turn, can irritate the bladder causing more frequent wetting. However, do be selective about what you give your child to drink. Milk and water are the best choices – avoid fruit juices and fizzy drinks.*

▶ *A water bottle in the car is a good idea, especially in hot weather.*

▶ *Whenever you have a stop (and try to have one about every one and a half hours) take your child to the toilet and encourage her to have a wee.*

Top tips for holidays

▶ *Once you have arrived at your holiday destination, make it your first priority to show your child where the toilet is or, if she is still using a potty, take it out and put it where she can find it.*

▶ *When on holiday most parents tend to be a little more lax about what their children drink. Do be aware of this and realize that if your child has recently trained and is not used to drinking lots of fruit juice or fizzy drinks, it may impact on her and she may be more prone to accidents.*

▶ *A change of routine or environment can sometimes lead to constipation, so keep an eye on your child's toilet habits.*

▶ *Also, a change in diet can lead to constipation. If your child is prone, take a supply of fresh fruit or dried fruit and her favourite breakfast cereal with you.*

▶ *Be aware that you may be out a lot more and finding a handy toilet is not always possible. Taking a fold-away potty may be the answer to that problem.*

Family upsets

All families have their crises; it is part of life's ups and downs. It is important and healthy for children to learn to deal with unexpected stresses. It will equip them with skills to cope in later life. Having said that, children do need to be protected and supported at these times.

Top tips for dealing with family upsets

▶ *Children tend to pick up quite quickly when there is a crisis of some sort in the family. Although it is tempting to think it is kinder to keep them in the dark, this can often misfire and make them even more anxious. You don't need to give them a blow-by-blow account of what is happening, but do give them an edited version so that their imagination does not run riot. Even worse, they may think that whatever is going on is their fault, so keeping them in the picture is usually a good move.*

▶ *Whenever possible keep your child's routines in place. When there is a family upset it can be very hard to stay focused on the children and it is a time when you can often let the routines go, but keeping the routines in place will reassure your child and will give her a sense of security. Often, it is at times of insecurity that children will feel the need to exert some control over their surroundings and this is when they may start to wet or soil.*

▶ *Try to continue to do the things that you normally do, like activities. Where possible, keep things normal.*

▶ *When you are under stress it is easy to let boundaries slip. But this is the time when young children need to know more than ever where they stand. So, however difficult, keep up the boundaries.*

▶ *Children often pick up on adult stress and it is not uncommon for them to regress in an area of development. They may become more clingy, anxious or even start wetting. It is important to remember that they are not doing this on purpose. It is a sign that they are feeling stressed and as such you need to respond to those clues.*

▶ *If you find that your child is wetting and you feel that a family upset may be at the root of it, review the problem thoroughly. Have you discussed the upset with your child? Keep it simple, but make sure she does not think it is her fault. Keep routines in place: it will give your child a sense of security. Maintain all your usual boundaries around behaviour – don't let them slip. Where possible try to keep life 'normal', doing your child's usual activities and routines. If this simply is not possible, explain to her why things have changed so that she does not think it is her fault. If she is wetting, remember the golden rule of not getting cross, clean her up and get on with life.*

▶ *Empathize with your child; let her know that you understand how she is feeling. Give her the space to talk. Bath time is always a good time to chat about the day or any worries she may have.*

▶ *Talk about the wetting with your child; she may be able to explain why it is happening.*

▶ *It may be a phase your child is going through and when the family upset has resolved, the wetting will also resolve. If you find it does not, then do seek further advice. Your GP is a good source for referral. With a younger child you may want to discuss it with your health visitor, and for an older child the school or school nurse will be able to help you gain further support.*

Summary

No one's life runs smoothly; there are always little upsets along the way. It is normal and healthy for children to react to new situations. This chapter will have given you lots of ideas to help with the changes that may happen in young children's lives. The main principles are to keep routines and boundaries in place, and keep talking to your child and reassuring her.

10 THINGS TO REMEMBER

1 *It is not uncommon for a child who has been dry for some time to have a relapse – there is usually a simple reason.*

2 *One of the most common reasons for a child to have a relapse is when a new baby arrives in the family – never a good time to start toilet training. If a child who has been doing well begins to have accidents check the list of tips to give you ideas on coping.*

3 *Remember never to get cross as it can be counterproductive and may lead to the issue continuing for longer than need be.*

4 *When children are unwell it is not uncommon for them to wet. If this happens it is always a good idea to get their urine tested to make sure they do not have an infection.*

5 *Moving house can be an enormous stress for children and they may regress. Involve your child in the move as much as possible so that she understands what is happening and why.*

6 *Starting school or nursery is another enormous event for your child. Again, preparation is all-important. Talk to her about what will happen. There are some great books on the market to share with your child.*

7 *Going on holiday often means a change of routine and unfamiliar surroundings and children can find this a challenge, increasing the chance of toileting accidents. Keep to their usual routine as much as possible and make sure that you show them where the potty or toilet is as soon as you arrive.*

8 *Children are often very sensitive to family upsets. They need to be supported and protected just like the rest of us.*

9   *Children do not regress or have a relapse without good reason and often this is something simple. Think about what is going on in their lives and what you can do to support them.*

10 *If your child has been toilet trained but has a relapse it is tempting to put her back in nappies but do try to avoid this. This situation will resolve itself much more quickly if you just continue with her toileting routine.*

Taking it further

Websites

GENERAL INFORMATION

www.nhsdirect.nhs.uk
Telephone number 0845 4647
Advice and health information service available 24 hours a day via the Internet and telephone.

www.gosh.nhs.uk
Information for children and families on health matters from Great Ormond Street Hospital.

www.eric.org.uk
Education and Resources for Improving Childhood Continence
ERIC Helpline 0845 370 8008: Monday to Friday 10 a.m. to 4 p.m.

BEDWETTING

www.stopbedwetting.org
A website that gives parental information on bedwetting and has a useful wetting questionnaire.

www.eric.org.uk
This website is for young people aged 13 to 17 in the UK who are experiencing bedwetting, daytime wetting, constipation or soiling.

THREADWORMS

www.fredworm.co.uk
The Threadworm Action Panel.

COMMUNICATION SYSTEMS

www.widgit.com
Widgit is a system of symbols to help children with physical or learning disabilities to communicate.

www.pecs.org.uk
Picture Exchange Communication System for children with autistic spectrum disorders.

www.makaton.org
Makaton uses signs and symbols to teach communication skills.

www.do2learn.com
Do2Learn provides pictures to help children to sequence a routine.

DISABILITIES AND PROBLEMS

www.nas.org.uk/earlybird
Earlybird programme – a course arranged by the National Autistic Society.

www.cafamily.org.uk
Contact a family – a UK-based charity giving advice for parents of disabled children. They are able to put such families in touch with other families in similar situations.

Further reading

I Want My Potty by Tony Ross (Andersen Press Ltd).

Potty Poo-Poo Wee-Wee by Colin McNaughton (Walker Books Ltd).

My Potty Book for Girls (Dorling Kindersley).
My Potty Book for Boys (Dorling Kindersley).

Waiting for Baby (All Day Long) by Frank Endersby [Child's Play (International) Ltd].

I'm a Big Brother by Joanne Cole (Eos).
I'm a Big Sister by Joanne Cole (Eos).

I Want a Sister (a Little Princess Story) by Tony Ross (Harper Collins).

Topsy and Tim Start School by Jean and Gareth Adamson (Ladybird Books).

Starting School by Alan and Janet Ahlberg (Puffin Books).

Elimination Problem: Enuresis and Encopresis. Behavioural Assessment of Childhood Disorders by D.M. Doleys *et al*.

Good Practice in Continence Services by Department of Health (Stationery Office).

THE TEACH YOURSELF RANGE OF PARENTING BOOKS:

Baby Massage and Yoga by Anita Epple and Pauline Carpenter.

Andrea Grace's Gentle Sleep Solutions by Andrea Grace.

Happy, Healthy Weaning Your Baby by Judy More.

Boost Your Baby's Development by Caroline Deacon.

Index

....

Image credits

Front cover: © Vadim Ponomarenko/Alamy

Back cover: © Jakub Semeniuk/iStockphoto.com, © Royalty-Free/Corbis, © agencyby/iStockphoto.com, © Andy Cook/iStockphoto.com, © Christopher Ewing/iStockphoto.com, © zebicho – Fotolia.com, © Geoffrey Holman/iStockphoto.com, © Photodisc/Getty Images, © James C. Pruitt/iStockphoto.com, © Mohamed Saber – Fotolia.com